Mackinac Connection:
The Insider's Guide to Mackinac Island

Third Edition

Amy McVeigh

Mackinac Publishing
Mackinac Island, Michigan

For information, write:
Mackinac Publishing, P.O. Box 215, Mackinac Island, MI 49757

© 1998 by Amy McVeigh

Printed in the United States of America

10 9 8 7 6 5 4 3   05 04 03 02 01 00 99 98

ISBN 0-9623213-3-8

Library of Congress Cataloguing-in-Publication Data

McVeigh, Amy, 1961–
    Mackinac Connection: The Insider's Guide to
        Mackinac Island/Amy McVeigh–3rd ed.
        p. cm.
    Includes bibliograhical references and index.
    ISBN 0-9623213-3-8
    1. Mackinac Island (Mich. :Island)–Guidebooks. I. Title.
F572.M16M38   1998   92-23695
917.74'923–dc20

🌺 🌺 🌺

Cover artwork by Martha Dunham. Copyright, The Gallery, 1987. Reprinted with permission.

When it went to press, the information in *Mackinac Connection: The Insider's Guide to Mackinac Island* was complete and verified through independent research and contact with businesses. But change reaches even Mackinac Island, so it's best to confirm all information before making decisions.

If you love this book and want to order copies for all your friends (don't loan them yours, buy more!), please see page 143.

❧ ❧ ❧

FOREWORD

Dear Mackinac Traveler:

You will love Mackinac Island. Having spent summers here for over twenty years, I have explored every corner and seen it during all seasons. I've introduced countless friends to its treasures and watched them begin to share my love for the island. Now I want to guide you around Mackinac Island's shores and through its woods.

All the guidebook basics are here: the hotels, the restaurants, and the shops. There are lots of tours, maps, and photographs, too. But the real fun comes with the offbeat information: why bats are good and bicycle flags are bad, how to act like a local, and what to take home as a souvenir. Whether you are planning your first trip to this magical island, or are under its spell and returning for the tenth time, **Mackinac Connection** *has something for you.*

— Amy McVeigh

❧ ❧ ❧

DEDICATION
AND ACKNOWLEDGMENTS

This book is dedicated to my daughters,
Shawn McVeigh-Braun, Jordan Lee Braun, and
Madison Lee Braun.

Shawn will never know the wonder of a Mackinac Island
summer, but her brief life taught us so much. Jordan and
Madison continue to delight and amaze with their
questions, curiosity, and sheer joy of living.

❀ ❀ ❀

Thanks to everyone who made
Mackinac Connection
a reality:

- All the readers of the early editions who gave me such great feedback and encouragement. The book and gift store buyers on and off Mackinac Island who understand the need for this book and sell it enthusiastically.

- My parents who introduced me to this marvelous place. My mother, Kate McVeigh, without whom the third edition wouldn't have happened. She had the tenacity to retype the book when the electronic file disappeared into cyberspace and she provided valuable insights based on her years on the island. Ann Woodman for racing through a fact checking trip. Len Trankina from the Mackinac Island Chamber of Commerce who calmly answered my endless questions. Joy McCoy for fielding calls from buyers and bookstores.

- Loretta Crum, who brought these pages to life with her clever design, and Sam Spiegel, from Partners Book Distributing, who believed in this book before I believed in him and has been a constant support ever since.

- My husband, Jeff Braun, for everything. Even putting up with me writing this third edition while we are in the midst of moving to Switzerland for a new adventure! My dad, Hugh McVeigh, for filling book orders while we are out of the country.

TABLE OF CONTENTS

Maps

Features:

Photo Credits:

Jeff Braun: 6, 7, 11, 20, 25, 26, 28, 31, 35, 40, 43, 46, 54, 65, 69, 74, 111, 119, 129, 131, 135, 137
Grand Hotel: 18, 57
Terry Phipps/Mackinac Island Chamber of Commerce: 5, 126
Mackinac Island Chamber of Commerce: 47
Mackinac Island State Park Commission: 84, 86, 92, 94, 95, 97, 102, 121
Michigan Travel Bureau: 39, 87, 104, 112, 124
Mission Point Resort: 22

1

Why You Should Come

"*Mackinac, as a health resort, is unsurpassed. Its cool air and pure water, together with its natural beauties and historic association, are just what are needed to bring back the glow of health to the faded cheek, and send the warm currents of life dancing through the system with youthful vigor. In Mackinac, you eat with a new relish, and sleep as when a child. You row, you ramble like boys and girls, scarcely able to keep your buoyancy within bounds. You need to set a double guard upon your dignity, lest it escape you entirely.*"

– From travel brochure of 1879

Mackinac is a timeless place. The peacefulness that goes with living in a horse-drawn world is evident immediately. Patient horses with fancy rigs are tied up outside the post office. Because there are no mailing addresses, all residents pick up their mail at the post office. Here gossip is exchanged, and notices of meetings are posted on the bulletin board. A clock on a cottage kitchen wall reads beneath the hands, "WHO CARES?" No one, that's who.

Mackinac is a humorous place. The beginning of the tourist season is ceremoniously marked each spring when the pool tables, a mainstay of the island winters, are removed from the year-round taverns. The smell of fudge intermingles with the aroma of the residue of horse-drawn carriages, creating an aromatic comedy. One cottager listed her dog in the phone book and made a daily trip to Doud's grocery store for ground steak for the pooch. On Halloween, the adults wear costumes and prowl the downtown.

Mackinac is a beautiful place. As the brochures accurately claim, Mackinac Island is a jewel in the sparkling waters of Lake Huron. Its majestic cedar-covered cliffs contrast with an endless blue sky. The air is clean, and the woods are overflowing with wildflowers. Waves ranging from calm to crashing hit the rocky beaches and send spray flying. Sailors, naturalists, golfers, romantics, and artists of every bent revel in the island's beauty.

Mackinac is a gentle place. People smile and say "hello" whether they know you or not. Stories exist of cottage owners inviting total strangers in to tour their spectacular Victorian homes. Couples of all ages stroll the boardwalk, holding hands beside the lapping waters.

A Mackinac vacation is a different kind of vacation. This isn't Palm Springs, where the weather is guaranteed and the shopping is fine. And it isn't New York City, with a quick cab ride to a foxy restaurant. Mackinac is contained, and the choices are limited. But the payoff is great for those who are ready to explore and enjoy.

🌸 🌸 🌸

Let's go ramble!

2

When to Come

Mackinac Island's tourist season used to be short: the Fourth of July to Labor Day. But that is changing. Families with school-age children still tend to visit during this time period, but others are finding that spring, fall, and winter are ideal times to find good rates and fewer people on their favorite island. Many people are surprised to find out that most hotels are open from mid-May through mid-October and that some are open all year.

Pick Your Season

Spring is the ideal season for nature lovers to visit. The trillium carpet the woods, and jack-in-the-pulpits raise their interesting heads. Wildflower varieties number in the hundreds here, and most of them make their initial appearance in the spring. Visit in the spring and you'll also witness the island hustling to get ready for the summer onslaught.

Summer is for tourists. All the shops, restaurants, and attractions are open and sailboats crowd the marina. The 500 horses that make everything happen work the streets. The cannon at Fort Mackinac booms every hour while guides describe the island's rich history.

Fall is for island aficionados. The trails are especially beautiful when the few hardwoods change color and contrast against the continual green of the cedars. Many of the businesses are still open, and the pace changes dramatically as the tourist season winds down.

Winter is a story unto itself. If you are one of those adventurous, slightly foolhardy, tougher-than-nails people who already loves Mackinac Island, try it in the winter. It is a pristine winter snow world, with great cross-country skiing and winter hiking. Turn to page 126 to learn more.

Weather or Not

Hey, it's Michigan. Northern Michigan. On an island. That means unpredictable, rapidly changing weather. Daytime summer temperatures are at least ten degrees cooler than in Detroit or Chicago. A hot, humid summer day in the Lower Peninsula can bring on fog that surrounds the island like a blanket. And the nights are cool, even in the summer. So be a good scout and come prepared for anything, all the time.

To learn more, check the five-day forecast for the island on the island's website at www.mackinac.com. Then remember how reliable forecasts are and pack everything anyway.

Events Worth Planning Around

The three Straits area communities (Mackinac Island, St. Ignace, and Mackinaw City), have a continuous calendar of interesting annual events. Following are the time-honored, well-attended yearly events that you might want to plan around. The dates vary yearly, so check in with the chambers of commerce before you firm up your plans. (See page 130).

MAY

Mackinaw City Pageant. On Memorial Day weekend, Mackinaw City residents don historically accurate costumes and replicate the pageantry and tragedy of life at Colonial Michilimackinac based on actual events that occurred from 1715 to 1763. Festivities also include a parade, fashion show, and fireworks.

JUNE

Mackinac Island Lilac Festival. In early to mid-June, Mackinac Island hosts a ten-day celebration of its abundant lilacs. The island has the oldest living lilacs in the United States, and its Lilac Festival is considered one of the top 100 tourist events in the nation. Highlights include outdoor concerts, a culinary delight called the Taste of Mackinac, walking tours guided by island insiders, and a parade.

Straits Area Auto Show. On the last weekend in June, St. Ignace plays host to a huge antique auto show. Thousands of old car lovers throng into town, either driving their own classic automobiles or just coming to look and admire.

JULY

Fourth of July. Mackinac Island, Mackinaw City, and St. Ignace all have celebrations and fireworks. Fort Mackinac and the Grand Hotel have special activities for children and adults.

Horse hitches dominate at the island's Lilac Festival parade.

Port Huron to Mackinac and Chicago to Mackinac Yacht Races. These two sailboat races are held back-to-back the second and third weekends in July. The fleets number just short of 300 most years. Multiply that by the number of crew on each yacht and you have quite a party for two weeks! The island gears up for the revelry by adding extra police and vast quantities of food and drink.

AUGUST

Horse Show. This August event, usually held in the middle of the month, is primarily geared to the island's year-round and summer residents. As a spectator event, it gives visitors a glimpse of the private world of islanders and their trusted steeds.

Antique Boat Show. During the second weekend in August, the Les Cheneaux Islands in Michigan's Upper Peninsula play host to a large antique boat show. From Mackinac Island, the Arnold Ferry Company takes a day excursion to the show.

Yachts jam the island's harbor during the annual boat races.

SEPTEMBER

Bridge Walk. On Labor Day, Michigan's Governor leads 40,000 to 60,000 walkers across the five-mile span of the Mackinac Bridge. Each person to finish receives a certificate of merit and a sense of accomplishment. You go at your own pace, and this event is attended by folks of all ages and ability levels. Two lanes of the four-lane bridge are closed to traffic to accommodate the walkers, so avoid the bridge on Labor Day if you are trying to get across quickly.

Mackinac Island Road Race. The first Saturday after Labor Day, the island hosts a walking and running race around its perimeter.

❀ ❀ ❀

In addition to these community special events, the Grand Hotel and Mission Point Resort frequently sponsor special activities. Annual favorites include Jazz Weekend, Somewhere in Time Weekend, and an Antique and Design Show at the Grand. Contact the hotels for more details.

Spring is a wonderful time to explore the island's beauty.

3

Getting Here

Mackinac Island lies between Michigan's Lower and Upper Peninsulas. You can get here three ways: by ferry boat from Mackinaw City or St. Ignace, by commercial or private plane, or by private boat.

Driving to the Mainland

The majority of island visitors drive to the closest point on the mainland, Mackinaw City from the south or St. Ignace from the north, and then take a ferry over to Mackinac Island. But if you haven't driven across the Mackinac Bridge, do it. This magnificent structure spans the Straits of Mackinac, where Lake Michigan meets Lake Huron. The bridge toll is nominal and the drive only takes an extra ten minutes or so.

Driving Distances to Mackinaw City

FROM	MILES
Chicago	390
Cleveland	430
Detroit	280
Lansing	225
Milwaukee	360
Petoskey	40
Sault Ste. Marie	62
Traverse City	100

Ferrying Across the Waters

Three ferry companies operate between Mackinac Island and the mainland: Arnold Ferry Company, Shepler's Ferry, and Star Line Ferry. All three operate from both Mackinaw City and St. Ignace. There are plenty of signs in those towns to direct you to the ferry docks.

Ferries run from May through October from Mackinaw City, and May through New Year's Day from St. Ignace. During the summer season, boats run about every half hour from 8:00 a.m. to 7:00 p.m.; there's often later service too, a big help if packing the van takes longer than you expected. In the off-season, boats are less frequent. Contact the ferry companies or the Mackinac Island Chamber of Commerce for the latest scheduling information.

Rates for 1998 are standardized at $13.00 per adult round trip and $7.00 for children (ages 5 through 12). Children under five are free. There's no additional charge for luggage, but taking your bicycle costs $5.75.

Whichever ferry company you choose, make sure to see that your luggage gets on the boat on the way to the island. When you reach the island dock, you'll need to identify your luggage and arrange for transportation to your hotel or bed and breakfast. The hotels have dock porters who meet the boats and assist with luggage and directions. You'll be amazed by how much luggage they can carry on a bicycle. Be sure to tip generously; porters work hard to make your arrival trouble-free.

If you read the billboards along the freeway near the island, you'll realize how competitive the ferry business is. Everyone has the fatest, safest, largest, or "bestest" boats. You can't go wrong with any of the companies, but here are a few things you might want to consider:

Arnold Ferry Company (800/542-8528 or 906/847-3351). Arnold's catamarans are the newest type of boats plying the Straits to Mackinac Island. A constant dispute between the three ferry boat companies makes it difficult to ascertain which boat takes the least time to cross. If the "Cats" are not the fastest, they are very close to it. And the roominess of the two deck cabins make moving around the boat a pleasure. Arnold also has older, slower boats that take the overflow in summer and become the sole transportation after November. The catamarans take about 15 minutes to cross, and the older boats about 40.

Day parking is free on the Arnold Dock, but there is a minimal charge for overnight. Valet parking and inside garages are also available for an additional fee. When you arrive on the island, you will find yourself right in the middle of town, across the street from the Carriage Tour and Chamber of Commerce offices.

Shepler's Ferry (800/828-6157, 616/436-5023, or www.sheplerswww.com). Shepler's boats are all fast, and Bill Shepler and sons pride themselves on their efficient, user-friendly system of taking luggage, cars, and travelers to their appropriate destinations. Again, there is a fee for secured parking and valet service, but overnight and day parking are free for up to five days. Shepler's also has a service garage that can handle light maintenance and car washes. When you arrive on the Shepler's dock on the island, you'll be on the western end of town.

Star Line Ferry (800/638-9892, 906/643-7635, or www.mackinacferry.com). Star Line boats are readily identifiable by the vaulting rooster tail of water that jets from their sterns as they make their crossing. Star Line has one dock in Mackinaw City and two docks in St. Ignace. Day parking is free. They charge fees for overnight, indoor, secured, and valet parking. On the island, the Star Line dock is on the western end of town.

Dock porters shuttle luggage between the docks and the hotels.

Flying In

The Mackinac Island Airport (906/847-3231) has a 3,500-foot paved, lighted runway that sees plenty of traffic in the summer. There is a modest landing fee for private single-engine, or multi-engine craft, and there is plenty of tie-down space. Small jet planes also land here. The airport is located about three miles from downtown, so you'll need to take a taxi (horse-drawn, of course) from the airport to your final destination.

The only commercial airline coming to the island is Great Lakes Air (906/643-7165) out of the St. Ignace Airport. The planes carry five passengers plus the pilot and can scoot you across to the island in about five minutes.

Another option is to fly with Northwest Airlines (800/225-2525) or American Airlines (800/433-7300) out of Chicago or Detroit and tack on their shuttle service into Pellston, Michigan. Pellston is only 12 miles south of Mackinaw City, and you can arrange van service from Pellston to Mackinaw City with Wolverine Stages (616/539-7165). If you'd rather continue through the skies to the island, contact the aforementioned Great Lakes Air. They'll pick you up in Pellston and fly you to the island.

Once you decide how you'd like to fly in, contact the appropriate companies to make arrangements and obtain fares.

Captaining Your Own Craft

The Mackinac Island State Marina (906/847-3561) is a favorite spot for Great Lakes boaters. The state-owned marina's slips can accommodate up to 100 boats, and are full most of the season. Slips are assigned on a first-come, first-served basis. If the marina is full, you can anchor in the harbor or try the marinas in Mackinaw City or St. Ignace.

Boats are charged rentals on a per-foot basis for overnight stays. The maximum stay is four nights; then you're out and some other patient crew gets their chance. The rates vary depending on the size of the boat and are slightly higher than rates for other state-owned marinas. The fee includes water, electricity, and public rest rooms. Don't plan your boating vacation to the island in mid-July, though, because that's when the marina is filled with racing sailboats.

The marina is open from mid-May to mid-October. Gasoline, diesel fuel, and a pump-out station are available. The harbor is 10 feet deep.

4

Staying Here

Mention that you are staying on Mackinac Island, and people will assume you are staying at "the hotel," referring to Mackinac Island's grand dame of hotels, the historic Grand Hotel. Many believe it is the only alternative for travelers who want to enjoy the island for longer than a day trip allows. But there is a wide variety of hotels, bed and breakfasts, and condominiums to accommodate most budgets. There are 26 inns in all, with almost 1,300 sleeping rooms.

The chart on page 15 provides a summary of accommodation information and includes 1998 room rates, based on two occupants during the high season. Off-season and special package rates are often considerably lower than those listed. The map on page 16 shows the location of most of the hotels and bed and breakfasts. Be sure to confirm all the information when you call for reservations. Descriptions of each of the accommodations follows the map.

If you are interested in a longer stay on the island, see the chart on page 33.

You won't find a Sheraton or a Holiday Inn on Mackinac Island. All the inns are privately owned and many are managed by the owners and their families. Most of the inns are quite old, and age brings charm and some occasional inconveniences. Guest rooms have been updated in recent years, but air-conditioning, televisions, and telephones continue to be on the scarce side. If these conveniences are an important part of your stay, be sure to inquire ahead of time. Children are welcome at any of the hotels and most of the bed and breakfasts. Pets are more difficult to accommodate. Non-smoking rooms and inns are becoming more common, so if you are a smoker, be sure to clarify the smoking situation when you call.

Many of the inns sell out during the peak season, so you should make your reservations as early as possible. Reservations are taken year round. During the high season, some inns require a minimum stay of two nights. Acceptable forms of payment and cancellation policies vary, so inquire when you make your reservation.

"I think what makes Mackinac so special is the unique blend of the historically significant, the fact that automobiles are not allowed, the presence of horse-drawn vehicles, and frankly, the architectural and natural beauty of the buildings and the island itself.

As the president of the Grand Hotel, I am obviously biased, but I think a visit to our high tea, luncheon, or dinner is a necessity for the island visitor. I love the feel and look of our parlor because of the mix of formality and informal elegance. I like the colors, the music, and the food. And the luncheon and dinner are such events."

– Dan Musser III , Grand Hotel

ACCOMODATIONS BY CATEGORY

HOTELS

Hotel	Double Room Rate (low-high)	Number of Rooms	Phone Number
Chippewa	$105 - $330	61	800/241-3341
Grand (includes breakfast & dinner)	$320 - $580	330	800/33-GRAND
Harbor View	$125 - $265	60	906/847-0101
Iroquois	$78 - $350	47	906/847-3321
Island House	$100 - $400	97	800/626-6304
Lake View	$90 - $325	85	906/847-3384
Lilac Tree	$135 - $285	39	906/847-6575
Mission Point	$99 - $388	234	800/833-7711
Murray	$69 - $225	69	800/4MACKINAC
Pontiac Lodge	$65 - $130	10	906/847-3364
Stonecliffe	$95 - $325	56	800/447-1339
Windermere	$100 - $180	26	906/847-3301

BED & BREAKFASTS

All include breakfast as part of the room rate; most serve continental breakfast.

Bed & Breakfast	Double Room Rate (low-high)	Number of Rooms	Type of Bath	Phone Number
Bay View	$95 - $285	19	Private	906/847-3295
Bogan Lane Inn	$68	4	Shared	906/847-3439
Chateau Lorraine	$55 - $165	10	Private & Shared	906/847-3820
Cloghaun	$80 - $130	10	Private & Shared	888/442-5929
Haan's 1830 Inn	$80 - $150	7	Private & Shared	906/847-6244
Hart's Haven	$55 - $120	7	Private	906/847-3854
Inn on Mackinac	$79 - $250	44	Private	800/4MACKINAC
LaChance	$79 - $89	18	Shared	906/847-3526
Lilac House	$70 - $100	5	Private & Shared	906/847-3708
McNally Cottage	$35 - $110	9	Private & Shared	906/847-3565
Market Street Inn	$90 - $185	7	Private	906/847-3811
Metivier Inn	$105 - $255	21	Private	888/695-6562
Pine Cottage	$55 - $300	15	Private & Shared	906/847-382
Small Point	$65	6	Private & Shared	906/847-3758

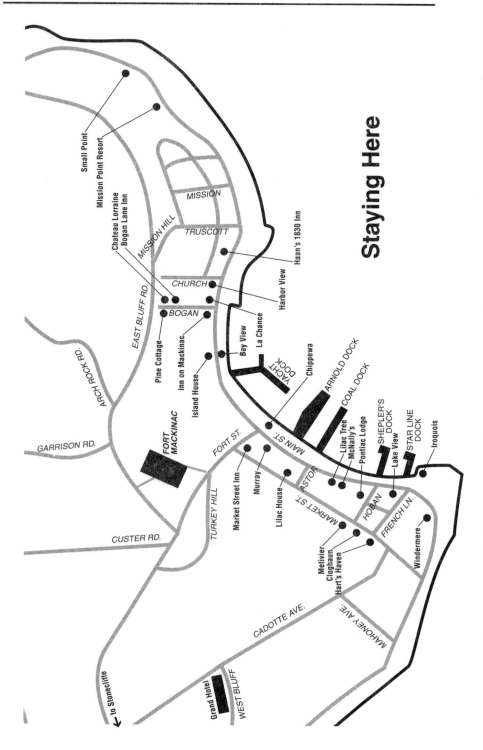

Staying Here

HOTEL DESCRIPTIONS

CHIPPEWA HOTEL
P.O. Box 250
Mackinac Island, MI 49757
800/241-3341
On Main Street at Fort Street. Open early May to late October. Rates are $105-$330 per room, based on double occupancy.

Located on the Main Street at the base of the Fort Hill, the Chippewa Hotel has been entertaining guests since the turn of the century. Because of its waterfront location adjacent to the marina, it is frequented by folks who love boats. The owners of the hotel began a massive renovation in 1993, converting its former 74 rooms into 54, and creating a large number of suites. The lobby and popular Pink Pony lounge were converted into larger restaurant space. The patio overlooking the lake is an extension of the restaurant, with lots of tables for drinking and dining. The former swimming pool on the patio has become a hot tub and waterfall, large enough for your family and most of your friends.

GRAND HOTEL
Mackinac Island, MI 49757
800/33-GRAND
On a hill about ½ mile northwest of downtown. Open early May to late October. Rates include breakfast and dinner and are $320-$580 per room, based on double occupancy. Additional surcharges apply.

People call the Grand "the hotel" on the island and honeymooners, political dignitaries, and conventioneers trip over one another to stay there. The Grand Hotel is billed as the world's largest summer hotel, featuring a 660-foot verandah overlooking the water.

Built in 1887 by a consortium of railroad and steamship companies seeking to increase vacation travel to northern Michigan, the Grand's success sparked the development of many of the large Victorian homes on the Island. A gamble at the time, the Grand is now a consistent success story; occupancy rates run over 90 percent. The hotel is owned by the Musser family, and they are building on a tradition of elegance that was set by Stewart Woodfill, a family member who gained ownership during the Depression.

Each of the rooms is decorated differently, under the careful eye of noted interior designer Carlton Varney. Many of the wallcoverings and fabrics

The Grand Hotel is the island's largest hotel, with 330 rooms.

were designed especially for the hotel. Notice the carpeting in the lobby that sports the hotel's trademark geraniums. You won't want to walk on it.

When guests tire of relaxing on the hotel's impressive porch, they may enjoy swimming in the serpentine pool, wandering through the spectacular gardens, golfing, playing tennis, or dining in one of the hotel's many restaurants (see Chapter Six). Most guests wear informal resort clothing during the day, but after six men are required to wear coats and ties (regardless of age) and dresses and suits are "preferred" for ladies.

Conventions are big business at the Grand; meeting rooms abound and the hotel has a full program of activities for adults and children.

HARBOR VIEW INN
P.O. Box 1207
Mackinac Island, MI 49757
906/847-0101
On Main Street, two blocks east of downtown. Open early May to late October. Rates are $125-$265 per double room.

A recent hotel conversion from a private home, the Harbor View Inn has a long and interesting history. The magnificent core home was originally built in 1820 by Madame La Framboise, a Great Lakes fur trader and granddaughter of Returning Cloud, Chief of the Ottawa Nation. When the Bacon Family bought the home in the mid-1990's, they set about designing a hotel around the original structure. They achieved fine results, and the hotel is now a coveted spot to spend nostalgic nights.

The 60 rooms and suites are delightfully furnished and feature fireplaces, jacuzzis, or lake views. Porches and white wicker abound. The public places are fine and large, including the lobby with its double fireplace, the dining room where breakfast is served, and the patio and private yard with its gazebo and hot tub.

IROQUOIS HOTEL
Mackinac Island, MI 49757
906/847-3321
On Main Street, at the west end of downtown, near the Shepler and Star Line docks. Open mid-May to mid-October. Rates are $78 - $350 per room, based on double occupancy.

Perched on the water's edge, the Iroquois rooms lay claim to the best view of the harbor, the Straits, and the Mackinac Bridge. The decor is stunning–

The Iroquois Hotel was transformed from a rectangular box into a building with interesting peaks, turrets, and porches.

island resort at its best. Each of the 47 rooms is decorated with a collection of wicker, wood, and flowery wall coverings.

Guests may enjoy the sunny three-room lobby, the front porch overlooking Main Street, and the back terrace near the shore. The Iroquois has an excellent restaurant (see Carriage House, in Chapter Six.)

ISLAND HOUSE
Mackinac Island, MI 49757
800/626-6304
On Main Street, just east of downtown and across from the marina. Open early May through late October. Rates are $100-$400 per room, based on double occupancy.

The Island House is the oldest operating hotel on the island, originally built in 1852. It has been expanded several times since then, and is registered as a Michigan historic site. Mackinac Island owes a debt of gratitude to the Ryba-Callawaert family for rescuing the structure in the 1970's when it was falling into disrepair. Extensive repairs and renovation have created a pleasant, historic hotel a short walk from the hubbub of downtown.

A new addition in the back of the hotel created luxury suites, an indoor pool, and a second restaurant. The back yard now features chairs for lounging or dining. Inside the main building, prices depend a great deal on location. Ask for a room with a lake view, and if you like cozy with dormers, try the fourth floor. The hotel has 94 rooms and three suites.

There is a two-room Victorian style lobby with a television for guests to use, but most spend their time on the verandah (second largest next to the Grand), overlooking the marina. The Governor's Dining Room and the Ice House restaurant are both described in Chapter Six.

LAKE VIEW HOTEL
P.O. Box 160
Mackinac Island, MI 49757
906/847-3384
On Main Street, between Hoban Avenue and French Lane. Open early May through mid-October. Rates are $90-$320 per room, based on double occupancy.

One of the newer old hotels, the Lake View sits on western end of town across from the Shepler and Star Line docks. The hotel originated in 1858, long before the Grand Hotel was constructed. In the 1980's, Harry Ryba had finished his Island House Hotel reconstruction and started in with vigor on the Lake View Hotel.

The result was an almost new hotel with 85 rooms, some with whirlpool baths. The most popular rooms are the tower rooms with their unique shape and pleasant view.

The Lake View has an enclosed, heated swimming pool. Its meeting rooms wrap around the pool. Beverages are available pool side, and meal service is available at two hotel restaurants (see James Cable Dining Room and Pilot House in Chapter Six).

LILAC TREE HOTEL
P.O. Box 540
Mackinac Island, MI 49757
906/847-6575
On Main Street, in the middle of town. Open early May to late October. Rates are $135-$285 per room, based on double occupancy.

The Lilac Tree Hotel brought the all-suites concept to the island. Sitting in the heart of the downtown area, with stores flanking the entrance, the yellow-and-white window awnings designate the location of the hotel.

The 39 suites in the hotel are tastefully appointed with imported furniture and accessories from France and England; no two rooms are alike. The parlor portion of the suites have sofa beds, in addition to the beds in the bedroom. All bathrooms are white marble with brass fixtures; some have jacuzzis. There are many extras–cable television, wet bar with refrigerator, coffee maker, and telephone.

The rooms in the front of the hotel have balconies overlooking the action on Main Street. Request a front room on the fourth floor for the best view. The hotel doesn't have a lobby for lounging in or a restaurant, but guests can wander through town and do either. Or both.

MISSION POINT RESORT
P.O. Box 430
Mackinac Island, MI 49757
800/833-7711
On Mission Point, about ¾ mile east of downtown. Open early May to late October. Rates are $99-$388 per double room.

Mission Point Resort is the island's second largest hotel.

After undergoing a multimillion dollar renovation, Mission Point Resort provides an alternative to the Grand Hotel for conventioneers and families looking for meeting space and full activities programming. The resort is located on 18 acres of waterfront property and offers 234 rooms and suites. Originally built by Moral ReArmament in the late 1950's and early 1960's, it briefly served as a college, and then struggled as a hotel in collegiate clothes for two decades until John Schufelt bought it and personally guided its transformation.

He kept what was good, such as the large timbered, cathedral-ceiling lobby, the 575-seat theater, and the many fireplaces. And he tore down, tore out, and redid the ugly. New features include 35,000 square feet of meeting space, landscaped grounds dotted with Adirondack chairs, a health club, children's activities center, heated outdoor swimming pool, and hot tubs.

Rooms are available in two lodges: Main Lodge and Straits Lodge. There are guest rooms with lake or garden views, family doubles with two adjoining bedrooms, or carriage suites with bedroom and parlor. Recent redecorating created three types of decor: nautical, the lodge, and northern Michigan.

Three restaurants serve up food and entertainment (see Chapter Six), and children under 12 stay and eat free.

MURRAY HOTEL
P.O. Box 476
Mackinac Island, MI 49757
800/4MACKINAC
On Main Street, in the middle of downtown. Open mid-May to mid-October. Rates are $69-$225 per double room.

The Murray Hotel has been offering friendly, family-style service to island visitors since 1882. It has maintained its Old World charm while updating its rooms.

Most of the 69 rooms are decorated with antiques and have pleasant touches such as lace swags over the beds. Some of us still miss the large lobby and restaurant with "windows on the world," but these have given way to retail space. Guests can buy fudge in the lobby all day long!

PONTIAC LODGE
P.O. Box 495
Mackinac Island, MI 49757
906/847-3364
On Hoban Street just north of Main. Open year-round. Rates are $65-$130, based on two occupants.

Pontiac Lodge is geared to the traveler who is planning a longer stay on the island. Its ten efficiency rooms are newer, clean, and utilitarian. They have refrigerators, sinks, microwave ovens, stoves, private baths, color televisions, and telephones. Coin laundry is available, and the coffee pot is always on in the morning.

STONECLIFFE RESORT
P.O. Box 338
Mackinac Island, MI 49757
800/447-1339
On the western bluff of the island, approximately two miles from downtown. Open mid-May through mid-October. Rates are $95-$325 per double room or condominium.

If your Mackinac vacation is designed to be a "get-away-from-it-all," Stonecliffe may be the perfect spot for you. Located on 175 acres high on the western bluff of the island, Stonecliffe is a retreat from the hustle of downtown Mackinac Island. The English Tudor mansion was built in 1904 as a summer home for the Cudahy family of Chicago, and was converted into a hotel in 1977.

The mansion has 14 rooms, all with private baths. The public areas and rooms are decorated beautifully with lots of antiques. Guests tend to spend lots of time on the back verandah, enjoying the view and quiet. Breakfast is available in the dining room each morning for an additional charge.

In an "only on Mackinac Island story," the Grand Hotel took over the restaurant on the Stonecliffe grounds and renamed it the Woods (see Chapter Six). The Grand's second nine-hole golf course is adjacent to the Stonecliffe property. Bike rentals are available on property, as is an outdoor swimming pool (not heated). Hiking and bike trails abound.

Stonecliffe's location two miles from town is either one of its best virtues or its biggest down side, depending on your point of view. The hike, bike, or taxi ride from the resort to town is beautiful and its location off in the woods creates a peaceful backdrop for an island getaway. But if you have to be in the middle of things, look elsewhere.

Stonecliffe Resort also rents out privately owned condominiums on the grounds. There are 43 condos in all, and about half of them are available to rent. The condominiums are right on the bluff, and most have spectacular views. A range of accommodations is available, from private bedrooms to bi-level three-bedroom suites with kitchens, fireplaces, patios, and solariums. Condominium information and rental is available through the resort or from these other sources:

- Bridgeview Condos   800/655-5740
- Island Time Vacation Rentals
  (has winter rentals too)   800/585-4053
- Joe's Island Getaway   800/631-5767
- Lakebluff Studio Suites   800/699-6927
- Pinewood Condos   906/847-3729

WINDERMERE HOTEL
P.O. Box 538
Mackinac Island,MI 49757
906/847-3301
On Main Street, at the west end of downtown. Open mid-May to mid-October. Rates are $100-$180 per double room.

The Windermere Hotel was originally built in 1887 as a private cottage.

Staying at the Windermere means staying at one of the historic summer homes on the island. The hotel was purchased by the Doud family at the turn of the century and has been operated by the family ever since. Pictures in the lobby show some changes through the years, but the original aura is retained due to the consistent hospitality of the Doud family

Each of the 26 rooms is decorated differently, many with antiques and wicker. Guests may enjoy a breathtaking view of the Straits from the white wicker-filled verandah, or on cooler days, warm up in the quaint three-room lobby. Continental breakfast is served daily in the sun room. Many rooms have views of the Straits, or of the Windermere's extensive garden.

BED AND BREAKFAST DESCRIPTIONS

BAY VIEW AT MACKINAC
P.O. Box 448
Mackinac Island, MI 49757
906/847-3295
On Main Street, just east of downtown. Open early May to late October. Rates are $95-$285 per room, based on double occupancy.

Bay View at Mackinac was built in 1891 and extensively renovated 100 years later.

Bay View's location at the water's edge near the marina is hard to beat. Innkeeper Doug Yoder, whose family has owned the building for years, capitalized on the location in a recent renovation and created 19 cozy rooms, most with water views and all with private baths.

Guests are encouraged to use the porches, sun deck, dining room, and living room. Continental breakfast is served in the dining room and punctuated by pots and pots of Bay View's own Mackinac blend coffee.

BOGAN LANE INN
P.O. Box 482
Mackinac Island MI 49757
906/847-3439
On Bogan Lane, one long block east of downtown. Open year-round. Rates are $68 per double room.

After the Martin family raised their children on Mackinac Island, they decided to turn their family home into a bed and breakfast so they could share it. The home was built in the 1850's and has four bedrooms to rent.

The Martins call the furniture in the rooms "island furniture" rather than antique, but most of it has been in the home for years. The rooms have a warm, homey appearance and share two modern baths. The back bedroom has a charming adjoining sun porch that has two twin beds and is ideal for children.

CHATEAU LORRAINE
P.O. Box 1888
Mackinac Island, MI 49757
906/847-3820
On Bogan Lane, one long block east of downtown. Open mid-May to mid-October. Rates are $55-$165, based on double occupancy.

Chateau Lorraine is named for its proprietor Lorraine Kingma. The home was built at the turn of the century and served as a private home until it was converted to its present use.

There are 10 rooms, some with private baths. Lorraine welcomes "well behaved children," and provides cribs and toddler beds. Continental breakfast is served in the dining room or in the courtyard gardens, weather permitting. Fans of the movie *Somewhere In Time* will enjoy seeing the piano featured in the movie and now housed in Chateau Lorraine's parlor.

CLOGHAUN

P.O. Box 1540
Mackinac Island, MI 49757
888/442-5929
One block north of town on Market Street. Open early May to late October. Rates are $80-$130 per double room.

Cloghaun (pronounced Clo-han) is Gaelic for "land of little stones." It is owned by James Bond (really!), a descendent of the Donnelly family, who left Ireland during the potato famine and built the home in 1884. Extensive renovation in the mid-1990s created a grand front porch and large public areas for guests to enjoy.

The inn has 11 bedrooms, most with private baths. Many of the rooms connect and can be rented as suites for families. Recent redecorating emphasizes the home's history while improving comfort and enjoyment.

HAAN'S 1830 INN

P.O. Box 123
Mackinac Island, MI 49757
906/847-6244
Three blocks east of downtown on Huron Street. Open mid-May through mid-October. Rates are $80-$150 per room, based on double occupancy.

Haan's 1830 Inn is the oldest building used as an inn.

As the name implies, the main building of this inn was built in 1830. It was later the residence of Colonel Preston, one of the last officers at Fort Mackinac, and mayor of the island at the turn of the century. With the 1847 addition, the inn has seven bedrooms, each named after a famous island person and beautifully decorated and furnished with period antiques. Some rooms share baths and others have private baths.

Continental breakfast is served daily in the dining room, and guests are welcome to enjoy the inn's three porches and the front parlors.

HART'S HAVEN
P.O. Box 266
Mackinac Island,MI 49757
906/847-3854
On Market Street at French Lane. Open year-round. Rates are $55-$120 per double room.

This motel look-alike is another Market Street bed and breakfast. Hart's Haven has four small rooms, and the furnishings are functional. Each room has its own bathroom with a shower. There is also an efficiency apartment available on a weekly basis.

INN ON MACKINAC
P.O. Box 476
Mackinac Island, MI 49757
800/4MACKINAC
On the corner of Main Street and Bogan Lane, one long block east of downtown. Open mid-May to mid-October. Rates are $79-$250 per room, based on double occupancy.

The Inn on Mackinac is the island's famous "painted lady." Like many of the island's larger structures, she served as employee housing for years, and then did a stint as a tourist home. But extensive renovations and 12 colors of paint gave the Inn on Mackinac new life as a 44-room inn with a colorful personality. When the paint job first got under way, there was a hue and cry from island politicos and residents. Now there is only hue, and a lovely thing it is.

Each of the rooms is furnished with antiques and has a private bath. Guests can enjoy the wrap-around porch, patio, and parlor with a fireplace. Some rooms have balconies.

LaCHANCE COTTAGE
P.O. Box 55
Mackinac Island, MI 49757
906/847-3526
On Main Street at Bogan Lane, one long block east of downtown. Open year round. Rates are $79-$89 per double room.

Built as a private home before the turn of the century, LaChance now rents its 18 rooms to the public. They are functional and clean. All share baths; some have sinks in the room.

LILAC HOUSE
P.O. Box 1267
Mackinac Island, MI 49757
906/847-3708
One block north of town on Market Street. Open mid-May through early October. Rates are $70-$100 per double room.

Across from the Post Office on Market Street, the Lilac House is another converted home. Its best feature is an innkeeper who was born on the island, and whose great-great-grandmother was born here too. Mary Thompson has owned the 1890s house for thirty years. She turned it into a five-bedroom bed and breakfast in 1992. There's a mix of shared and private baths.

MARKET STREET INN
P.O. Box 315
Mackinac Island, MI 49757
906/847-3811
At the corner of Market and Fort Streets. Open mid-May through mid-October. Rates are $90-$185 per room, based on double occupancy.

Market Street Inn is, appropriately enough, located on Market Street, which used to be Mackinac's main street. Historic buildings line Market Street, and the Inn is no exception. There are seven bedrooms, furnished with antiques.

Rooms have cable television and private baths. Guests are welcomed in the small lobby and are encouraged to "hang out" on the little front porch. Or they can walk right across the street to Marquette Park where a lot of "hanging out" goes on.

McNALLY COTTAGE

P.O. Box 366
Mackinac Island, MI 49757
906/847-3565
On Main Street, between Astor and Hoban Streets. Open late May through mid-September. Rates are $35-$110 per room, based on double occupancy.

The McNally family has been welcoming guests to Mackinac Island for more than 100 years. McNally Cottage's nine rooms are simple, clean, and homey. Some of the rooms have private baths, and others share a bath. Guests can watch the Main Street activity from the privacy of the enclosed front porch, while enjoying a continental breakfast.

Metivier Inn was transformed from a house into a large bed and breakfast.

METIVIER INN
P.O. Box 285
Mackinac Island, MI 49757
888/695-6562
On Market Street, between Astor and Hoban Streets. Open mid-May through late October. Rates are $105-$255 per double room.

Metivier Inn is a charming Victorian-style inn with 21 rooms. Most of the inn was built in 1984 but with its architecture and location on historic Market Street, it has the aura of a much older establishment.

The rooms are beautifully decorated, mostly with new wicker and brass furnishings. Two rooms have antique furniture. For a special occasion, ask for one of the two turret rooms. Each room has a private bath. Guests are free to enjoy the large front porch to watch the constant parade of people, horses, and bikes go by.

PINE COTTAGE
P.O. Box 519
Mackinac Island, MI 49757
906/847-3820
Open mid-May to mid-October. On Bogan Lane, one long block east of downtown. Rates are $55-$300 per double room.　　'

Pine Cottage was built in 1890 as a boarding house and retained its boarding house feel and budgetary appeal until 1998 when Lorraine Kingma, proprietor of Chateau Lorraine across the street, took over, and began sprucing up.

The Cottage offers fifteen rooms, some with private baths, and an apartment loaded with beds for your family reunion. Public areas include a living room, dining room, and a large porch facing Bogan Lane.

SMALL POINT
P.O. Box 427
Mackinac Island, MI 49757
906/847-3758
About ¾ mile east of downtown on Huron Street. Open early May through Labor Day. Rates are $65 per double room.

Pedal past Mission Point Resort on the east end of town, and you will find yourself in front of Small Point, a pleasant alternative to the downtown inns. Small Point was built in 1882 as a private summer house, and has a lovely view of the water.

Most of the rooms share baths. Ask for one of the rooms with a lake view, or enjoy the view from the wicker-filled porch or deck. A television is located in the living room, along with VCR and games. There is always a jigsaw puzzle underway, and a piano waiting to be played. Bicycles are available for the guest to use.

COTTAGES, APARTMENTS, AND HOUSES

Availability of cottages, apartments, and houses varies considerably year to year. Here are some that are frequently available. Contact the Mackinac Island Chamber of Commerce (800/4-LILACS) or Mackinac Island Realty (906/847-6483) for the most up-to-date information. Also see the description of Stonecliffe Resort on pages 24-25, where a number of condominiums are available.

Name	Double Room Rate	Phone Number
Bay Cottage	House with weekly rate	906/847-3401
Great Turtle Lodge B&B	$150 - $240	800/206-2124
Harbor Place Apartments	$75 - $240	800/626-6304
Island Time Vacation Rentals	$135 - $395	800/585-4053
Jenny Wren Apartments	$100 - $125	906/847-6125
North Star Inn	$100 - $175	906/847-3263
Silver Birches	House with weekly rate	906/847-3238
Tulecki Apartments	Weekly or monthly rate	906/847-3489
Voyageur Inn Apartments	$159 - $238	906/847-6175

5

Getting Around

When visitors arrive on Mackinac Island for the first time, they are struck by what is not present: cars. Instead of the noise and smell of the horseless carriage, there is the noise and smell of the horse-drawn carriage.

Motor vehicles have been banned on the island since the turn of the century when they were just appearing on the American scene. A group of entrepreneurs who made their living driving carriages and freight-hauling drays on the island were concerned that the automobile could force them out of business. They successfully petitioned the City Council to ban motorized vehicles. Little did the City Council know then that job preservation action would ultimately lead to preserving the island's appeal.

Exceptions to the ban are made for public safety vehicles, including a motorized ambulance, police jeep, and fire engine. During the off season, businesses can request a permit for construction vehicles. And in the winter, island residents and visitors use snowmobiles as their primary transportation.

Without cars, your main mode of transportation on the island will be your feet. A bicycle can help. Or, for a price, a horse-drawn carriage will take you where you want to go.

Your Feet Can't Be Beat

Walking is the easiest, least expensive, and in most weather, the best way to see most of Mackinac Island. Wear comfortable shoes, and don't be lulled into a false sense of security because there are no cars. Getting run over by a bicycle or a horse isn't a great way to spend your vacation. See Chapters Eight and Nine for suggested walking tours of natural and historical attractions, and Chapter Ten for tours designed with exercise as the priority.

For those who need additional assistance, adult strollers and mobility carts are available through some bike rental companies. See page 38.

Tandem bicycles are easy to ride as long as you don't
try to steer from the back!

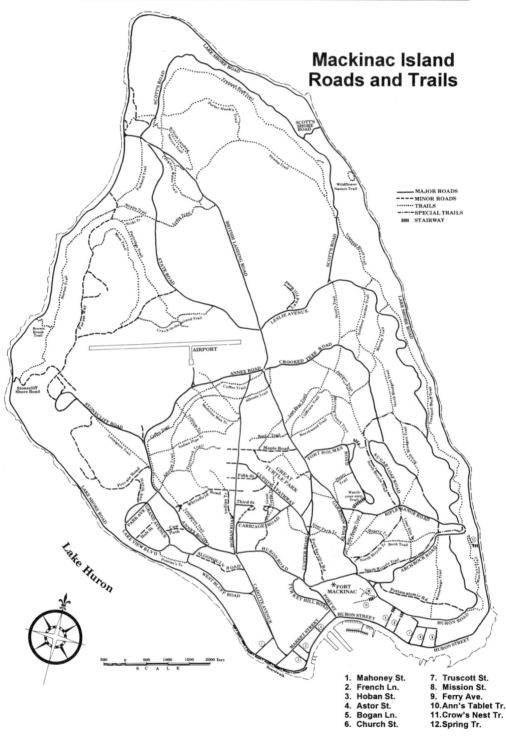

Mackinac Island
Roads and Trails

——— MAJOR ROADS
----- MINOR ROADS
·········· TRAILS
—··—··— SPECIAL TRAILS
ⅠⅠⅠⅠ STAIRWAY

Lake Huron

SCALE
500 0 500 1000 1500 2000 feet

1. Mahoney St.   7. Truscott St.
2. French Ln.   8. Mission St.
3. Hoban St.   9. Ferry Ave.
4. Astor St.   10. Ann's Tablet Tr.
5. Bogan Ln.   11. Crow's Nest Tr.
6. Church St.   12. Spring Tr.

Cycle Central

If you plan to do much biking, take your own bike to the island. The ferry companies charge a fee for bikes, but that will be quickly offset with savings in bike rental charges. If you have a bicycle flag, take it off or wrap the flag around the pole and secure it. These flags tend to spook the horses. It's a good idea to bring your lock too. Mackinac Island is nearly crime-free, but there are always people who think it is a lark to jump on an unlocked bike and joyride for a time. Avoid these hassles by keeping your bike locked.

Whether you bring your own bike or rent one, wear a bicycle helmet. You might want to bring your own helmet, although they are available from some of the bike rental companies.

Rental bicycles are available from nine rental companies on the island. Hourly rates vary from year to year and depend on the type of bicycle you rent. But rates are reasonable, beginning at about about $5 an hour for a basic bike. If you plan to ride all day, ask for a day rate. A deposit is required for all rentals. Most of the rental companies do not take credit cards, so bring your cash.

Rental bikes range from two-speed models (stop and go), to 21-speed mountain bikes. Child seats are available, as are small bikes for children, regular tandems, mini-tandems (adult on front, child on back), tagalongs (single wheel attachments for a child on the back of an adult bike), and Burley-type carts (two-wheel carts for children attached to an adult bike). If you want one of these specialized bikes, go early to get it. Rental outlets open in season at 8:00 a.m.

Remember when you are riding that the rules of the road apply, even though there are no cars. The roads are crowded, and many people haven't ridden a bike in years. Follow these guidelines for everyone's safety:
- Wear a bicycle helmet.
- Ride on the streets, not sidewalks or boardwalk.
- Stay to the right of the road.
- Give horses the right-of-way.
- Watch for pedestrians that forgot to watch for you.
- Do not make abrupt turns without looking around you.
- Do not read historical markers while in motion.
- Do not stop your bicycle in the middle of the road.
- Do not ride double, ever.

The island's terrain creates a few areas that are not safe for bicyclists. Walk your bike down Turkey Hill, between the Governor's summer residence and the Grand golf course, and down Fort Street, from the Governor's to Marquette Park. Be careful when going down the Grand Hotel Hill and Mission Hill; they are deceptively steep. Bike riding is prohibited on the marina walks and the boat docks to limit unintentional swimming.

Park your bicycle in designated areas downtown; yellow curbs indicate the no-parking zones. If you leave your bike on the street downtown after 3:00 a.m., it may be impounded. The streets are cleaned during those hours with high-powered hoses.

Bicycles that will be on the island all summer must be licensed at the Police Station. If you bring your own bike to the island, a portion of the fee you pay the ferry company goes for a visitor's bike license. These license fees help fund bike safety efforts.

Chapter Ten has bike routes designed for exercise and sightseeing, or create your own route from the map on page 37.

Rental bicycles are available at the following locations:
- Iroquois Bike Rental next to Shepler dock, 847-3321 (will repair bikes for guests of the Iroquois Hotel)
- Island Bicycle Livery near Shepler dock, 847-6288
- Island House Rentals at Island House Hotel, 847-6261
- Lake Side Bikes at Arnold Line dock, 847-3351 (takes credit cards)
- Lake View Bikes across from Lakeview Hotel (also rents child strollers and mobility carts)
- Mission Point Bikes at Mission Point Resort, 847-3312
- Orr Kids' Bikes near Shepler dock, 847-3211, (takes credit cards and also rents adult and child strollers)
- Ryba Bikes next to the Pancake House, 847-6261 (also rents child strollers)
- Street Side Bikes next to taxi office, 847-3351 (takes credit cards)

A Surrey with the Fringe on Top

A surrey with the fringe on top is a favorite for all ages, and is available in many forms on Mackinac Island. On a first visit to the island, take a carriage tour. These tours provide a good introduction to the island, exposing you to many sights and stories.

***Mackinac Island is one of the few places in the country
where three-horse hitches are used.***

PRIVATE CHAUFFEURED CARRIAGE

Private chauffeured carriages are available by the hour on Main Street in front of Marquette Park. Rates are about $15 an hour per person based on a minimum of four people and a maximum of seven. These colorful rigs line up by the park, and the loaders explain the service and rates and team you up with strangers if you don't have a minimum party of four. If you wish to reserve ahead, call Arrowhead Carriages at 847-6112, Carriage Tours at 847-6152, or Gough at 847-3391.

Many of the guides are long-time island residents, happy to answer all your questions in addition to giving you a guided tour. Tell them what you'd like to see, and they'll design a tour for you. Otherwise, they'll tell you what you'd like to see and take you there. Either way, you'll enjoy it. My favorite route is to go in front of the Grand Hotel, past the west bluff, through the Annex and Harrisonville, past the Governor's summer residence and Fort Mackinac, past the east bluff and back to the park.

GROUP CARRIAGE TOUR

Group tours are available from Carriage Tours (847-3325) on Main Street right across from the Arnold Line dock. The tour lasts just under two hours and the rate is about $13 for adults and half that for 4-11 year-olds.

Your littlest ones can tour free. After boarding a 20-passenger carriage, you will ride through town and up the Grand Hill to a museum and shop area, where you'll transfer to a three-horse, 35-passenger wagon for most of the tour.

Your driver will give you an overview of the island's history and many of the sights, including Market Street, the Grand Hotel, Arch Rock, and Fort Mackinac. The driver gives passengers an opportunity to disembark at Fort Mackinac, the Grand Hotel or return downtown.

DRIVE-YOURSELF CARRIAGE

Jack's Riding Stable (847-3391), around the corner from the French Outpost on the Grand Hill, rents horse-drawn carriages that you can drive yourself. Prices vary, but you can figure about $34 an hour for one or two people and go up from there. The company harnesses up the horse to the cart, walks you out to the road, suggests trails that are interesting (and that the horse will agree to), and sends you on your way. Take a sense of adventure, a lot of patience, this book, some snacks, and your strongest "giddyup" voice.

*A drive-yourself carriage is a relaxing way to explore
the island's interior.*

Hail That Cab

If "taxi" evokes an image of hailing a beat-up Plymouth with a lighted sign on top and speeding from point A to point B, forget it. Taxis on Mackinac Island are radio-dispatched horse-drawn carriages that seat 12. They are as much entertainment as they are transportation. Sometimes they come on time, sometimes they don't come on time, and sometimes they don't come at all.

Taxis operate 24 hours a day, seven days a week during the season. If you are in a busy area, you can approach a taxi driver who will call in to request a taxi for you. If you are downtown, stop at the taxi office on Main Street at the foot of Astor Street. Or call 847-3323 to talk to the taxi dispatcher. The route often resembles a milk run, so plan in advance if you need to be somewhere at a specified time.

Rates are in zones, per person, with a minimum of two people for longer runs. Taxis do not transport bicycles or unaccompanied luggage. There is an additional charge for luggage in excess of three bags per person.

"What makes Mackinac Island so special is that it combines the low-key ease of the nineteenth century with the convenience of the twentieth.

If you visit, don't walk in the streets. The island is becoming more popular and this increases the danger of pedestrians being hit by bikes and horses."

— John McCabe
Author and island resident

A Horse of Course!

Horses provide the power on Mackinac Island: they taxi visitors from ferries to hotels, move freight from docks to businesses, deliver the mail from the plane and boat to the post office, and even pick up garbage. Horse people who visit the island are amazed by the skill and the diversity of the 600 horses it takes to keep the island working in the summer.

More than half of the horses are owned by Carriage Tours, which puts them to work in two- or three-horse team carriage tours, drays, or taxis. The carriage tour and dray horses are heavy draft horses, capable of pulling heavy loads. They are Percheron, Belgian, and Clydesdale mixes, from the Amish areas of northern Indiana.

For taxi horses, Carriage Tours selects lighter, quicker driving horses, usually Standardbreds or Standardbred crosses that aren't quite fast enough to make it on the racing track. The riding stables look for sensible riding horses of mixed breeding.

Horses bound for Mackinac Island make their first stop in Pickford, Michigan, the winter home of the island horses. There they are trained for island duty. The intricate process of carriage horse training begins with breaking one horse to drive, then matching it with an experienced horse. The trainers match the horses' gaits, colors, sizes, and temperaments. Then the team is matched with a driver. (Drivers are selected on the basis of their strength and ability to communicate with horses and people, and they participate in a minimum of two weeks of training.) The team is ready after the horses are brought to the island and exposed to all sorts of situations that can arise when there are so many horses, bicycles, and people in one location.

Horse lovers sometimes worry that horses on the island are overworked. That is very uncommon. Taxi horses have a four hours on, twelve hours off schedule, while carriage tour horses typically do not work more than five hours a day. The riding stable horses have the longest days, but rent one and you'll see that they are good at making sure they don't work too hard!

Keeping all the horses in footwear is a real challenge. Saddle and taxi horses are shod with steel shoes that have borium tips. Steel shoes alone act like ice skates on pavement, so the borium is added, giving the shoes a cleat effect. The heavier horses are shod with a shoe specially designed for use on the island. It is steel, covered with polyurethane. It is extremely durable, and does not cause as much wear and tear on the

A Horse of Course! (cont.)

roads as the borium shoe does. There are four working blacksmiths on the island in the summer and one veterinarian.

The best spot to watch horses is at the top of the Grand Hotel hill. Grab a seat by the side of the road and watch all types of horses go by. Then stop at the Grand Hotel stables (across from the Jockey Club at the Grand Stand) and check out the horses and old carriages. Wander the rest of the way up the hill, past the Carriage Tour barns, to Surrey Hill. It has excellent displays of old carriages and harnesses and photographs of carriages in use. There's often a blacksmith shoeing a horse and a draft horse out for display.

There are two other unusual horse activities to watch. Look for a dray driver backing a team and a load of freight into a tight loading area. Could you do that with your car? Also look for horses coming over on the ferry on one of the Arnold Line Ferry freight boats. Most of them arrive in May and June, and depart after Labor Day. The day after Labor Day is the busiest, with up to 25 horses on one boat.

Horses get to the island the same way most visitors do—by boat.

6
Beyond Fudge

Vacations are about eating, at least part of the time. And planning where to eat and how to eat is one of the fun parts if you know the territory. This chapter will help you make tasty choices, whether you want to dine in stately surroundings or grab a slice of pizza to take to the park.

Mackinac Island's most famous food product is its fudge, but since one cannot live by fudge alone, there are lots of restaurants to serve visitors and island residents. Most of them are concentrated downtown, but there are others outside of town.

Attire in Mackinac restaurants is casual, with the exception of the Grand Hotel restaurants in the evening. Reservations are rarely required, except as noted below. Most establishments except the snack shops take credit cards, but if you are low on cash, ask before you order. Most restaurants on the island have children's menus.

The description of restaurants that follows is divided into three parts: (1) downtown restaurants, (2) restaurants outside of downtown, and (3) Grand Hotel restaurants. Liquor availability is indicated under the name of the establishment, as well as price ranges for dinner entrees (excluding beverages and appetizers).

DOWNTOWN RESTAURANTS

Main Street on the north side, beginning at the east end near Marquette Park

GOVERNOR'S DINING ROOM–ISLAND HOUSE HOTEL
906/847-3347
Breakfast, lunch, dinner, and evening entertainment. $18-$28. Full bar.

In the oldest hotel on the island, the Governor's Dining Room blends a pleasant decor with a harbor view and evening entertainment. Breakfast is a buffet, catering largely to hotel guests. Dinner is the time to go, and the food is excellent. The bar sort of blends into the dining room, and the entertainment is enjoyed by the entire room. Large windows overlook the marina and the stars at night.

ICE HOUSE BAR & GRILL–ISLAND HOUSE HOTEL
906/847-3347
Lunch and dinner. $6-$9. Full bar.

Hidden next to the swimming pool behind the Island House Hotel, the Ice House Bar & Grill promises to be a fun place off the beaten path. Soups, salads, sandwiches, and burgers are served up for lunch and dinner inside or out, weather permitting.

3 BROTHERS SARDUCCI
906/847-3880
Lunch and dinner. $4-$10.

Mackinac Island's answer to Little Caesars, the 3 Brothers have expanded and spruced up in recent years. The focus is on pizza and spaghetti, but sandwiches and other items are available too. Dine in on the checkered covered tables or carry out to a favorite spot.

Some visitors still prefer fudge.

PUB OYSTER BAR AND GRILL
906/847-3454
Breakfast, lunch, dinner, and evening entertainment. $6-$20. Full bar.

The Pub Oyster Bar and Grill is billed as an 1890's saloon, and the tin ceilings, wooden bar, and historic memorabilia set the tone. It is housed in a very old building, and has a nice intimacy. The menu is large and varied, from burgers to omelettes. It's one of the few places on the island where you can get baked brie if the needs strikes.

HORN'S GASLIGHT BAR
906/847-6154
Lunch, dinner, and evening entertainment. $5-$14. Full bar.

Owners Patti Ann and Steve Moskwa recently updated the decor at this long-established restaurant bar. Horn's is known as the place to be at night, but during the day it is a very popular place to get a sandwich, burrito, or hamburger. A sing-along type piano player entertains the lunch crowd, and a get-right-down-to-it band entertains the crowd after 9 p.m.

***Dining at the Tea Room at Fort Mackinac offers
a view, history, and tasty treats.***

TY'S RESTAURANT
906/847-3426
Breakfast, lunch, and dinner. $4-$9. Full bar.

If you're looking for an inexpensive meal with no frills, check out Ty's. The menu is primarily sandwiches, burgers, hot dogs, and chicken, served in baskets with french fries. They brag about the early-day Bloody Mary, so don't be shy about ordering one.

WATERS MEET
906/847-3806
Lunch, dinner, and evening entertainment. $6-$17. Full bar.

Down the stairs by the Lilac Tree Hotel, this restaurant is the below sea level eatery that its name suggests. The theme is carried out everywhere; custom murals on the walls, models of Great Lakes ships and lighthouses. Proprietors Mark and Tom Sposito are well-known for their restaurants in St. Ignace, and they bring to Waters Meet the sense of good food for a reasonable price. Whatever floats your boat in the food line, they have.

JESSIE'S CHUCK WAGON
906/847-3775
Breakfast, lunch, and early dinner. $3-$9.

This is a 1950's type diner with most of the seats at the counter. Jessie doesn't mean to be putting on a show; she is just getting folks their food. But she does put on a show. A favorite breakfast spot for locals, there is a whole lot of information floating down the counter.

PILOT HOUSE–LAKE VIEW HOTEL
906/847-3384
Lunch and dinner. $6-$20. Full bar.

The Pilot House is a large, family-style restaurant serving sandwiches and more substantial American fare. Its window seats are a great place for people watching.

JAMES CABLE DINING ROOM–LAKE VIEW HOTEL
906/847-3384
Breakfast and dinner. $17-$27. Full bar.

The Lake View Hotel's James Cable Dining Room serves regional cuisine in a formal (for Mackinac) setting. Prime rib is a specialty. Window seats overlooking Main Street are great fun, particularly as the night goes on!

Starting on Main Street near Fort Street, on the south (lake) side

HARBORSIDE DINING ROOM AND PINK PONY– CHIPPEWA HOTEL
906/847-3341
Breakfast, lunch, dinner, and evening entertainment. $15 -$25. Full bar.

During a renovation at the Chippewa Hotel, the popular Pink Pony bar, the dining room, and related areas were combined and now all serve from the same menu. Service continues onto a large outdoor patio overlooking the harbor, which makes this a good bet on nice days. And the food is worth the trip even when the weather isn't so nice.

PANCAKE HOUSE
906/847-3829
Breakfast and lunch. $4-$8.

For an inexpensive breakfast served in a plain brown wrapper, the Pancake House is a good choice. It offers breakfast fare all day, and adds a sandwich menu at lunch.

WATERFRONT CAFE
Lunch. $4-$8.

On the Arnold Line dock, the Waterfront Cafe has sandwiches, hot dogs, fries, and burgers available at a window with picnic tables in a sheltered area for seating.

SURREY SANDWICH SHOP
906/847-3743
Lunch and dinner. $5-$10.

For a quick submarine sandwich, it's hard to beat the Surrey Sandwich Shop. The Surrey also offers other sandwiches, salads, and homemade chili. Call, and they will prepare a picnic for your group.

MIGHTY MAC HAMBURGERS
906/847-3813
Breakfast, lunch, and dinner. $4-$7.

Mackinac Island is one place that Ronald McDonald hasn't discovered, so your kids may learn to like Mighty Mac's charbroiled hamburgers. The Mac also serve hot dogs, salads, and other similar fare.

MARTHA'S SWEET SHOP
906/847-3790
Light breakfast, sweets. $1-$3.

If you follow the early morning traffic, you are likely to end up at Martha's for one of her famous melt-in-your-mouth cinnamon rolls and large cups of coffee. Martha also makes muffins, brownies and cookies, and sells ice cream. Carry-out or sit at a counter.

MR. B'S
Lunch and dinner. $3-$6.

Mackinac's version of a Dairy Queen, Mr. B's serves ice cream treats, hot dogs, nachos, and other items from its window on Main Street. Picnic tables are available outside in the back to accommodate diners.

MOCHA JOE'S
906/847-0260
Breakfast, lunch, and snacks.

Tucked in the back of the Horse Corral Mall, Mocha Joe's is a small coffee house with a water view. The emphasis is on java, but pastries and sandwiches are also available. Limited seating.

ORR KIDS' SNACK SHOP
Lunch and snacks. $3-$6. Carry out only.

Orr Kids' has hot dogs, nachos, brats, ice cream, popcorn, and the like conveniently located next to its bicycle rental shop.

ISLAND CAFE AND ICE CREAM
Lunch and snacks. $3-$8

With two entrances, this combo affair includes cones, sundaes, malts and shakes, plus an interesting array of sandwiches made to order as you stand at the counter. A few indoor tables, and a very few outdoor tables.

DOCKSIDE RESTAURANT
Breakfast, lunch, and dinner. $4-$12. Full bar.

As the name implies, Dockside is right near the Star Line dock. Specializing in ribs and chicken, the restaurant has a strong nautical theme with ship models, maps, and other stuff. Dockside is home to the island's largest beer selection (more than 160 domestic and international beers at last count). If you have one of each, your name goes on a plaque over the bar. Not recommended for a four-day weekend.

LIGHTHOUSE GRILL
Lunch and dinner. $6-$15. Full bar.

Outdoors behind the Dockside and just off the Star Line dock, this restaurant is very pleasant. They cook on the outdoor grill and the food is limited but very tasty. Sometimes a local musician will set up and entertain the luncheon crowd.

THE CARRIAGE HOUSE–IROQUOIS HOTEL
906/847-3321
Breakfast, lunch, and dinner. $15-$28. Full bar.

The Carriage House is on everyone's list of best places to dine, so reservations are recommended for dinner. The view of the breakwater and the Straits is awesome, and the Mrs. Mac's special care is evident throughout. Try the grilled seafood sandwich for lunch, and the prime rib for dinner. Save room for the Mackinac Island Fudge Ice Cream Puff!

Downtown restaurants on the side streets

LETTERMAN'S ASTOR STREET CAFE
906/847-3252
Lunch and dinner. $12-$17. On Astor Street between Main and Market.

After years of working in other people's island restaurants, Tim McCleery seized the chance to make his own mark on Mackinac's culinary choices in 1988. He transformed a sandwich and ice cream shop into a fine Italian dining experience. The atmosphere is casual, with island scenes painted on the walls. The menu changes often, so stop in as ask Tim what he has planned during your stay.

MUSTANG LOUNGE
906/847-9916
Lunch and dinner. $4-$10. Full bar. On Astor Street between Main and Market.

The Mustang is a legend. Open all year, it is a favorite of locals who practically have their own bar stools, and start occupying them early. The food is served on paper plates and consists of simple stuff, like a grilled ham and cheese. The Mustang also serves tourists with friendliness, and its a good spot to get information since the wait staff are locals.

YANKEE REBEL
Lunch and dinner. $7-$23. Full bar. On Astor Street between Main and Market.

If it's been too long since your last island visit, you might find yourself in search of Little Bob's and its famous cinnamon rolls in this space. Forget Little Bob and meet Ambrose Davenport, an American who refused to swear allegiance to the crown during a British takeover of Mackinac long ago. Called the "Yankee Rebel" by the Brits, Davenport is celebrated in this red, white, and blue restaurant. The colonial feeling is accented by a large fireplace and menu choices that lean to hearty American fare.

VILLAGE INN
906/847-3542
Lunch and dinner. $7-$17. Full bar. On Hoban Street between Main and Market.

The V.I., as it is known to insiders, is a favorite watering hole for island people, and a favorite eating place as well. The planked whitefish surrounded by mashed potatoes and veggies is legendary. But all of the food is very good. There are cozy high-backed booths as well as alot of table space. And on nice days there is full food and beverage service on the front porch.

RESTAURANTS OUTSIDE OF DOWNTOWN

THE POINT DINING ROOM–MISSION POINT RESORT
906/847-3312
Breakfast and dinner. $15-$32. Full bar.

The Point Dining Room at Mission Point Resort has a vaulted pine ceiling, pleasant decor, and an entire wall of windows overlooking the Straits, so plan to spend some time in leisurely dining. Arrive hungry, because the menu focuses on big meats and seafood.

ROUND ISLAND BAR AND GRILL–MISSION POINT RESORT
Lunch, dinner, and evening entertainment. $8-$16. Full bar.

For a casual lunch or dinner and some freighter watching, the Round Island Bar and Grill at Mission Point Resort is a good bet. Sit around the circular bar, or at one of the tables around the hotel lounge. Service is also available outside when the weather cooperates. Easy listening entertainment most nights.

FREIGHTERS' DELI–MISSION POINT RESORT
Lunch and dinner. $4-$10.

Freighters' Deli is often overlooked, but it shouldn't be. Find it in the lower level of Mission Point Resort, and enjoy the usual deli fare of salads and sandwiches, complimented by nice breads and other baked items.

Many of the eateries offer outdoor dining when the weather is nice.

FRENCH OUTPOST
906/847-3772
Light breakfast, lunch, dinner, and evening entertainment. $7-$20.

Another local favorite, the O.P. doubled in size in 1998 and moved upscale from its position as a rock n' roll haven at night. Now jazz bands and more mellow entertainment reigns. Menu favorites such as oysters and clams from the raw bar and tasty sandwiches remain; new entrees move up from there and include specialties cooked on an grill outside. Large serving area inside and out.

TEA ROOM AT FORT MACKINAC
906/847-3347
Lunch. $5-$8. Beer and wine.

For a bird's eye view of the harbor, there is no finer place for a lunch on Mackinac Island than the Tea Room at Fort Mackinac. Operated by the Grand Hotel, the Tea Room serves soups, salads, and sandwiches outside under umbrellas or inside the old officer's "mess" with its fireplaces and beamed ceilings. You must pay admission to the Fort to eat in the Tea Room.

THE WOODS
906/847-3331
Dinner. $12 -$28. Full bar.

Another "Grand" experience away from the Grand Hotel, the Woods restaurant is a pleasant bike or carriage ride through the woods of the island's interior. This Bavarian lodge was built as a game room for the Cudahy children when the family lived at Stonecliffe Mansion in the early 1900's.

The beautiful restoration of the building, coupled with the out-of-the-way location and excellent food has made the woods a favorite for special occasions. If you want to get into the Bavarian spirit and eat brats you can, but seafood, steaks, and other fare rounds out the menu. Reservations are recommended.

JOCKEY CLUB
Lunch, dinner, and evening entertainment. $8-$26. Full bar.

The Jockey Club is located on the Grand Hotel golf course and is open to the public without the admission fee or dress code. Umbrella tables line the entrance and are usually full. There is an outdoor dining area that is protected from wind and weather in addition to the charming inside dining room. At lunch, the menu is salads and sandwiches; in the evening, the grill reins. So to speak. Usually in season there is an entertainer, playing piano or guitar. This is a very popular dinner spot for cottage-owners and other insiders.

J.L. BEANERY
Light breakfast, lunch, and snacks. $1-$7.

Conceived as an alternative to the evening bar scene, J.L. Beanery serves up a variety of coffees, teas, and hot chocolates day and night from a cozy location next to the marina. Enjoy your hot beverage with pastries in the morning, or desserts in the afternoon or evening. Some mellow entertainment sometimes.

BRIAN'S BARBEQUE
Lunch. $4 -$7.

If you are missing your grill while you are on the island, wander past the Island House Hotel toward Mission Point Resort, and you'll likely find Brian. Bicyclists are drawn to the curb if they are at all hungry. Brian serves hot dogs, brats, barbecued chicken, and conversation.

CANNONBALL
Snacks and lunch. $2-$6.

Halfway around the island, this little lunch window is an oasis to the hiker or biker. They have soda, snacks, and sandwiches.

GRAND HOTEL RESTAURANTS

In order to eat breakfast or lunch at any of the restaurants inside the Grand Hotel, you'll need to pay the $7 per person hotel admission charge. A portion of this charge is credited to your bill if you eat the luncheon buffet. At night, the price of admission changes to your attire–coat and tie for men (of all ages) and dress or pantsuits for women. Meal prices at the Grand restaurants include tips for the wait staff. Call 847-3331 for more information about any of the Grand restaurants.

GRAND HOTEL–MAIN DINING ROOM
Breakfast, lunch, and dinner. Buffet lunch $30; Sit-down dinner $65. Full bar.

For a step into the Victorian days of extravagant multi-course meals, the Grand's Dining Room at dinner is incomparable. Guests are ushered down an aisle way surrounded by pillars and mirrors as though in a fashion parade. The orchestra plays, and you order from a rotating menu that includes five courses. Lunch is also unique, because it is a huge buffet covering ten banquet tables filled with hot and cold entrees, salads, breads, and over 40 different desserts. Reservations recommended.

GRAND HOTEL–TERRACE ROOM
Entertainment and dancing. Full bar.

An elegant room for drinks and dancing, with no cover charge. The orchestra starts about 9 p.m., and the dance floor is big and popular. Just be sure to call ahead to make sure it isn't booked for a private party. With no admission fee at night, and no cover charge, this is the Grand's only bargain. Just be sure to dress to the nines.

The entrance to the Grand Hotel's Main Dining room is designed to create a promenade.

GRAND HOTEL–AUDUBON WINE BAR

With its dark green and maroon decor and nature theme, the Audubon Wine Bar has an exclusive hunt club feel. Its quiet, comfortable atmosphere is a welcome retreat from the afternoon and evening activity in the rest of the hotel.

GRAND HOTEL–CARLETON'S TEA STORE

Lunch and sweets. $7-$9. Beer and wine.

On the lower level of the Grand Hotel, Carleton's offers a limited menu of soups, sandwiches, and fruit and cheese trays, and an outstanding array of desserts. These are displayed in a carousel in the hallway, and prove too tempting for most visitors.

GRAND HOTEL–POOL GRILL

Lunch and snacks. $5-$9. Full bar.

A day at the Esther Williams pool is sure to include some food or beverage, and the Grand Hotel makes it easy from gazebo right on the lawn by the pool. Hot dogs, hamburgers, and chicken are prepared on grills. If you are not a guest of the hotel, there is a separate admission fee to the pool. So plan to go early and stay late.

GRAND HOTEL– GERANIUM BAR

Continental breakfast.

If you don't want to eat breakfast in the Grand's Main Dining Room, the Geranium Bar serves up a tasty continental breakfast. Add an excellent view of the Straits, and you are on your way to a good day.

GRAND HOTEL–CUPOLA BAR

Entertainment and dancing. Full bar.

The cupola on the top of the Grand Hotel is a two-story bar, with a dance floor on one level, and the band playing jazz, pop, or easy listening that can be enjoyed on both floors. With its commanding view of the Straits and a carnival feeling, the Cupola Bar is a fun place to spend an evening. Dress code applies.

NIGHTLIFE

Mackinac Island is not mid-town Manhattan, but, considering its size, the island has a fair amount of action after the sun goes down. If you haven't been out at night, you haven't seen all of Mackinac. Many of the bars that swing at night swing with live music, from full bands to individual entertainers. So come along on a night time tour; try these spots:

- Horn's Bar
- Waters Meet
- Pink Pony
- Mustang
- Village Inn
- J.L.Beanery
- The Pub
- Mission Point Resort
- Grand Hotel
- Jockey Club
- French Outpost
- Island House Hotel

Kids' Corner

Mackinac Island is an ideal family vacation destination. All the hotels, restaurants, and shops welcome children. You won't have any trouble finding high chairs or hot dogs, cribs or cots. And older children love the freedom that comes with being able to ride their bikes anywhere. There's plenty to keep kids of all ages busy. Some favorites:

Picnics: Load your bicycle basket with picnic foods and pedal to a special spot.

Fort Mackinac: Kids can play soldier on a grand scale. The musket and cannon firings are great crowd pleasers. And check out the children's discovery room, where children explore the sounds, sights, and feel of history.

Swimming: From swimming holes to swimming pools, it's all explained on page 115.

Playgrounds: There are playgrounds at the school, behind the Indian Dormitory, and at Great Turtle Park. Marquette Park, Windermere Point, Mission Point, and the grounds behind Fort Mackinac are good for running, jumping, and playing outdoor games.

Horses: Most kids love horses. Carriage tours, taxi rides, driver-yourself carriages, and saddle horses are all popular with the younger set. Chambers Riding Stable has pony rides for the really little ones. Most carriage drivers will let your children pet the horses or pose for a picture, but ask first (the driver, not the horse).

Biking: Family bicycle outings are easy and safe. See page 37 for details.

Butterflies: The Mackinac Island Butterfly House, located on the lane behind St. Anne's church, is a great place for children to explore. It's filled with butterflies and fragrant flowers.

Competition: During the Lilac Festival and the Fourth of July celebrations, there are competitive games for children.

Haunted Theatre: A favorite with the teenagers, the Haunted Theatre is on the west end of town, the north side. Even if you wait outside, you'll be able to hear the screams.

Kids' Corner (cont.)

Arcade Games: If the need strikes, check the list on page 129.

Movies: Monday night is movie night on the island. Family movies are shown at Mission Point Resort. Check the *Town Crier* or the Chamber of Commerce for information.

Other child-related tidbits:

The Grand Hotel and Mission Point Resort have full programming for guests' children.

Check at your hotel or the Chamber of Commerce for lists of babysitters.

You'll be doing lots of walking, so bring your stroller or rent one from Ryba's Bikes, Lake View Bikes, or Orr Kids' Bicycle Rental.

7

T-Shirts, Tomahawks & Treasures

Time was on Mackinac Island when about all you could purchase was a pound of fudge and a rubber-tipped tomahawk. Those honored traditions still exist, but the shopping scene has expanded in recent years. Now the diligent shopper can find all sorts of ways to spend money–fudge, T-shirts, fine clothing, watercolors, jewelry, and more.

You can search for treasures in three primary shopping districts: 1) Main Street between Fort Street and French Lane; 2) Market Street between Fort Street and French Lane; and 3) the Grand Hotel. Because there is so much to see on the island, and you won't want to spend all day shopping, I've included short descriptions of the shops to help you plan your time. About half of the shops listed have been doing business on Mackinac for years. The other half changes hands or merchandise fairly frequently, so if you don't find what you expect, enjoy the hunt.

Main Street Shopping

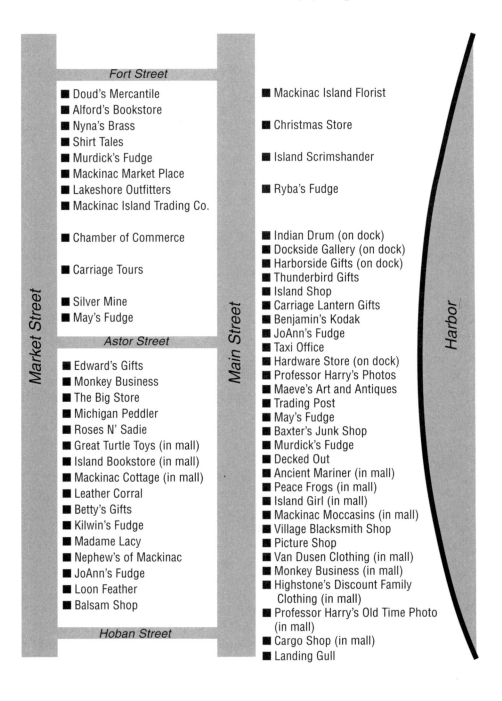

Fort Street

- Doud's Mercantile
- Alford's Bookstore
- Nyna's Brass
- Shirt Tales
- Murdick's Fudge
- Mackinac Market Place
- Lakeshore Outfitters
- Mackinac Island Trading Co.

- Chamber of Commerce

- Carriage Tours

- Silver Mine
- May's Fudge

Astor Street

- Edward's Gifts
- Monkey Business
- The Big Store
- Michigan Peddler
- Roses N' Sadie
- Great Turtle Toys (in mall)
- Island Bookstore (in mall)
- Mackinac Cottage (in mall)
- Leather Corral
- Betty's Gifts
- Kilwin's Fudge
- Madame Lacy
- Nephew's of Mackinac
- JoAnn's Fudge
- Loon Feather
- Balsam Shop

Hoban Street

Market Street

Main Street

Harbor

- Mackinac Island Florist

- Christmas Store

- Island Scrimshander

- Ryba's Fudge

- Indian Drum (on dock)
- Dockside Gallery (on dock)
- Harborside Gifts (on dock)
- Thunderbird Gifts
- Island Shop
- Carriage Lantern Gifts
- Benjamin's Kodak
- JoAnn's Fudge
- Taxi Office
- Hardware Store (on dock)
- Professor Harry's Photos
- Maeve's Art and Antiques
- Trading Post
- May's Fudge
- Baxter's Junk Shop
- Murdick's Fudge
- Decked Out
- Ancient Mariner (in mall)
- Peace Frogs (in mall)
- Island Girl (in mall)
- Mackinac Moccasins (in mall)
- Village Blacksmith Shop
- Picture Shop
- Van Dusen Clothing (in mall)
- Monkey Business (in mall)
- Highstone's Discount Family Clothing (in mall)
- Professor Harry's Old Time Photo (in mall)
- Cargo Shop (in mall)
- Landing Gull

MAIN STREET SHOPPING

Listed in order as you stroll down Main Street beginning at the corner of Main and Fort Streets. The north side is listed first, followed by the south side (lake side) of Main Street.

Shops on the north side of Main Street, beginning at Fort and Main.

DOUD'S MERCANTILE
Doud's is the island's only grocery store and has been serving island residents and tourists since the 1840's. For a small town grocery, it has a wide selection. Open all year.

ALFORD'S DRUG STORE
Another island institution, Alford's has been dispensing prescriptions and other necessary items to island residents and visitors for years. They can have prescriptions filled for you on the mainland, and they also have a wide variety of souvenirs and gift items. Open all year.

NYNA'S BRASS
Wear your sunglasses when you walk into Nyna's or you'll be overcome by all the gleaming brass pieces. Nyna carries a huge array of brass items from an inexpensive key chain to a big bucks engine room telegraph for a ship. Although there is something for almost everyone's taste, many of the pieces have a nautical theme.

SHIRT TALES
One of the first island shops to carry higher quality island theme merchandise, Shirts Tales carries contemporary casual clothes for men and women, almost all emblazoned with "Mackinac Island." You'll also find jackets, sweatshirts, and rain gear here.

MACKINAC MARKETPLACE, LAKESHORE OUTFITTERS, AND MACKINAC ISLAND TRADING COMPANY
The success of a single store in the Murray Hotel in the mid-1990's prompted a cloning effort of these stores, which are jointly owned and carry a similar merchandise of monogrammed, high quality clothing. Shirts and jackets range from T-shirts to denim to thick fuzzy stuff.

*The Main Street Centre Mall is the newest addition to
Mackinac's shopping district.*

SILVER MINE
Once a treasure of silver, the Silver Mine moved away from its mainstay
and into T-shirts, sweatshirts, hats, and other souvenirs, with a little bit of
silver mixed in.

EDWARD'S GIFTS
Primarily a souvenir shop, Edward's can surprise the diligent shopper with
its collection of bone china and Hummel figurines. It also carries shoes,
raincoats, and hats for those caught on the island without the essentials.

MONKEY BUSINESS
One of a relatively new pair of stores, Monkey Business means business
when it comes to Mackinac Island T-shirts and sweatshirts.

THE BIG STORE
A souvenir lover's delight, the Big Store is the biggest of the traditional
island shops. It carries all the favorites: T-shirts, sweatshirts, tomahawks,
hats, wind-up toys, and other trinkets.

MICHIGAN PEDDLER
The Michigan Peddler brings a wealth of Michigan talent to Mackinac Island. The store's tribute to Michigan includes photography, pottery, books, wind chimes, wooden toys, and other delightful gift items. You can stock up on Michigan jams, jellies, and wines too.

ROSES N' SADIE
Named after two special grandmothers, Roses N' Sadie has fine gifts. German ornaments, table linens, and travel bags are carefully displayed alongside a variety of collectibles.

GREAT TURTLE TOYS (in the back of the Lilac Tree mall)
Ben Nye, who for a long time had a kite store on the island, has taken over the island's only toy store. The result? Kites, windsocks, and the like join a nice collection of toys and games.

ISLAND BOOKSTORE (in the back of the Lilac Tree mall)
A must for travelers who enjoy books, the Island Bookstore has a fine selection of best-sellers, regional books, activity books and kits for children, and other titles to make your vacation even more relaxing.

MACKINAC COTTAGE (in the back of the Lilac Tree mall)
The sounds and scents of Mackinac cottage life hit you as you enter this spacious shop. The walls and shelves are covered with fine throws and pillows that accentuate the Victorian lifestyle. Quilted articles are everywhere, along with some glassware and china.

LEATHER CORRAL
As the name implies, the Leather Corral specializes in leather goods, including wallets and purses, moccasins, belts, and duffel bags. It also has numerous horse figurines, Indian toys, and beaded necklaces.

BETTY'S GIFTS
Along with the usual souvenir items, Betty's Gifts carries knives for sporting activities and other surprising merchandise.

MADAME LACY
With a line of Victorian lingerie, the name of this new shop is self-evident. But the store also carries candles that smell marvelous, a line of lacy scarves, and some fine china.

NEPHEW'S OF MACKINAC ISLAND
Nephew's is the place to go when you didn't pack quite the right clothes for a special outing. It is a full-line clothing store for men and women featuring Liz Claiborne, Ralph Lauren, Nautica, and other name brands.

LOON FEATHER
The Loon Feather has an extensive selection of pewter figurine collectibles. In addition to moccasins and sweatshirts, it carries Hudson Bay woolens, sweaters and other items.

BALSAM SHOP
The Balsam Shop has the souvenir mainstays – T-shirts, hats, knives, and Indian trinkets. But because the T-shirts are hanging on the walls, it's easier to pick out your favorite. The shop also has a larger-than-most selection of Mackinac Island trays, mugs, trivets, and the like.

MACKINAC GEAR
The success of a single store in the Murray Hotel in the mid-1990's prompted a cloning effort of stores carrying monogrammed, high quality clothing. Shirts and jackets range from T-shirts to denim to thick fuzzy stuff.

Shops on the south side (lake side) of Main Street, beginning at Main and Fort.

MACKINAC ISLAND FLORIST
This is a full-service florist shop located in the Chippewa Hotel. With coolers full of flowers, they are prepared for weddings and special occasions. They even sell lilac trees! Part of the shop is devoted to information and gift items relating to the Butterfly House.

CHRISTMAS STORE

To get yourself in the festive spirit for shopping, stop in the Christmas Store. Ornaments, decorations, and gift items of the season abound. You may just find yourself doing your Christmas shopping in July!

ISLAND SCRIMSHANDER

For a fine gift for someone special (or yourself), check out the necklaces, earrings, rings, knives, belt buckles, and more at the Island Scrimshander. Each features island and nautical scenes meticulously created by an artist.

INDIAN DRUM

Tucked around the corner on the way to the Arnold Line dock, the Indian Drum derived its name from its authentic Indian-made replicas of Indian tools and instruments. It also carries higher end Mackinac Island gear and other gift items.

DOCKSIDE GALLERY

This small shop in the Arnold Line building carries framed photographs of island scenes and a selection of metal sculptures.

HARBORSIDE GIFTS

A T-shirt and sweatshirt kind of place, Harborside is really an extension of the Thunderbird shop next door.

THUNDERBIRD GIFTS

This store has some jewelry in the front, and loads of T-shirts and sweatshirts in the back. Good selection of children's tees.

ISLAND SHOP

A vast display of T-shirts and sweatshirts that boast of Mackinac Island makes up the majority of the Island Shop. But sprinkled here and there are ceramic miniature animals and larger figurines.

CARRIAGE LANTERN GIFTS
Carriage Lantern Gifts features a large selection of inexpensive jewelry, including nautical theme pieces and charms. Its Mackinac Island insignia items include T-shirts, mugs, ashtrays, hats, trivets, and magnets.

BENJAMIN'S OF MACKINAC ISLAND
Benjamin's biggest sellers are camera-related products – film, film processing, batteries, cameras, camera cases, and video supplies. And if you find yourself in a jam with a camera that doesn't want to work, Bob

Most of the island's shops are on Main Street.

Benjamin might be able to help you out. Benjamin's also carries an interesting selection of gift and souvenir items.

HARDWARE STORE (on the coal dock)
Operated by the folks at the Arnold Line, this place hums with activity all year long. From massive renovation supplies to the little screw that fell out of the toilet paper holder, your solutions are here in this surprisingly complete hardware store.

PROFESSOR HARRY'S OLD TIME PHOTOS
Slip on a costume from the collection and find yourself in the 19th century as a military man, a huckster, a Victorian lady, or a hussy. Photos are developed in authentic looking sepia tones while you shop the rest of Main Street. Remember, don't smile!

MAEVE'S ARTS AND ANTIQUES
After spending many summers on the island, Maeve decided to join the ranks of merchants seeking to enhance the island's shopping experience. And she's had success. Her shop features artful jewelry, ceramics, baskets, boxes, wind chimes, offbeat clothing, and other treasures.

TRADING POST
If you let your young children in the Trading Post, you'll probably lose them for hours; it is filled with the trinkets kids love to inspect. It also has an array of Mackinac Island T-shirts, hats, pot holders, and beach towels.

BAXTER'S JUNK SHOP
As the name implies, the items offered here will appeal to a child's sense of Mackinac souvenirs. Part of a family owned triumvirate of similar island stores, Baxter's had a moment of glory in the movie *Somewhere in Time*, when it was called Baxter's Coin Shop and was featured in a street scene.

FRANK SHAMA GIFTS
Now operated by Frank Shama's descendants, the Frank Shama Shop has been in existence of Mackinac Island for almost 60 years. While the most

popular items in the store are probably the souvenir items, the owners are justifiably proud of their fine china selection.

DECKED OUT

Featuring moderately priced men's and women's casual clothes, Decked Out can be counted on for the latest colors and designs in comfortable wear. If you are looking for a Mackinac memento to wear, but don't want a T-shirt, you might enjoy their polo shirts and sweaters.

ANCIENT MARINER (in the Horse Corral Mall)

A spacious shop at the back of the Horse Corral Mall, the Ancient Mariner carries gift items that have a nautical theme, from old schooners to today's slick sailboats. Pictures, throws, and artifacts pertain to the ships of the Great Lakes.

PEACE FROGS (in the Horse Corral Mall)

If you like frogs, this shop is for you. Frogs plus peace signs equals peace frogs. Right on.

ISLAND GIRL (in the Horse Corral Mall)

Since the demise of the island's only children's clothing store, Island Girl has picked up on that potential market, and features very sweet clothing for the young child. She also carries of limited supply of children's shoes and tasteful and fun gift items.

VILLAGE BLACKSMITH SHOP

Mackinac Island is known as the place where the horse is king, and the Village Blacksmith Shop pays homage to that king. You can have a souvenir horseshoe personalized with your name, or take home one of the many horse related items.

PICTURE SHOP

The Picture Shop carries a large selection of greeting cards, plus books on the history of the island and children's books. Sister shop to Benjamin's down the street, the Picture Shop will also have your film processed.

VAN DUSEN CLOTHING

Van Dusen Clothing carries T-shirts and sweatshirts with all sorts of mottos and logos, but nearly all bearing the Mackinac Island name too. A few gift items can be found, but the emphasis is shirts, shirts, and more shirts.

MONKEY BUSINESS

One of a relatively new pair of stores, Monkey Business means business when it comes to Mackinac Island T-shirts and sweatshirts.

PROFESSOR HARRY'S OLD TIME PHOTOS

Slip on a costume from the collection and find yourself in the 19th century as a military man, a huckster, a Victorian lady, or a hussy. Photos are developed in authentic looking sepia tones while you shop the rest of Main Street. Remember, don't smile!

HIGHSTONE'S DISCOUNT FAMILY CLOTHING

In this store, Highstone's, long a part of the island's retail scene, caters to the family that needs four T-shirts instead of one. They keep the prices low, and have a wide variety of products.

CARGO SHOP

The folks at the Cargo Shop proudly call their operation the "Cargo Shop Tourist Trap." Do I need to say more?

LANDING GULL

Keep up your stamina, because the last shop on Main Street is worth visiting. The Landing Gull offers an eclectic mixture of nautical gifts, Michigan artwork, and basic souvenirs. It also has attractive Mackinac Island note cards, prints, posters, and watercolors. Along with its sister stores on Market Street, the Landing Gull carries the island's largest selection of Cat's Meow Village wooden replicas of island scenes.

MARKET STREET SHOPPING

Listed in order as you stroll down Market Street beginning at the corner of Astor and Market and continuing to Market and the Grand Hill. This covers all of Market Street first, and then the connecting side streets.

Shops on Market Street, on the south side, except as noted.

GIFT HORSE

Right on the corner of Market and Astor, the Gift Horse's main theme is horses; they even sell chocolate horse suckers! The jewelry is interesting and ties into the island theme where possible. Look for the silver bicycle necklace.

PHOTOS ON MACKINAC

A swift, efficient photo shop for your quick development needs. The walls feature photos by long-time island photographer Rob Jerstrom.

THE BIRCHES

If you skipped the Main Street souvenir shopping scene, here's your chance on Market. The Birches is packed with merchandise, most of it with a Mackinac Island theme.

PAINTINGS BY WOLFGANG (across the street)

Richard Wolfgang, noted artist and Mackinac Island aficionado, brought his considerable talent to the island several years ago when he did a painting that was used on a Lilac Festival poster. He now has a gallery where his works can be viewed and purchased.

ROSE GAZEBO

This shop features merchandise with a Victorian flavor, yet it is mounted on standard fabrics like denim and T-shirt knits. There's a strong tie to Mackinac's past in this shop, with flowered china and lots of lace.

LANDING GULL

The sister store to the Landing Gull on Main Street, this store carries a nice selection of nautical gifts, Michigan artwork, and souvenirs. Look for the Mackinac Island cross-stitching kit and the Michigan related books. The Landing Gull carries the island's largest selection of Cat's Meow Village wooden replicas of island scenes – 22 and counting.

The most popular souvenir from an island visit is fudge,
handmade on marble slabs.

JAUNTING CART
Emily spent years on the island in various jobs before deciding to bring a bit of Ireland to Mackinac Island by opening this import shop. The Jaunting Cart features crystal, stoneware, woolens, and other gift items. Coats of arms for Irish family names can be reproduced immediately, along with family histories.

MACKINAC LAPIDIARY (in the Carousel Mall)
Frank Bloswick, Jr., part of a long-time Mackinac Island resident family, brings a new expertise to the island by cutting gem stones and doing glass engraving to order. The store also features fine crystal lamps and stemware.

NORTHWINDS (in the Carousel Mall)
Jim Lazarowicz, owner of Landing Gull Gifts on Main and Market, continues his niche as purveyor of Great Lakes area products and nicer souvenirs in this shop, which is tucked in the back of the Carousel Mall. This shop adds more sportswear, Christmas items, and northern lodge accessories to the mix.

LILACS AND LACE (in the Carousel Mall)
You can smell the theme of Lilacs and Lace as soon as you enter this store. All the lilac scents hit you at once; then you see the vintage linens, lace-covered photo albums, hat boxes, prints, and other items.

WEATHERVANES (in the Carousel Mall)
In the back of the Carousel Mall, Weathervanes' claim to fame is its ornamental working weather vanes. The store also features island and Great Lakes art and accessories and the wooden collectible series of island scenes from Cat's Meow Village.

TASSIA'S GIFTS (in the Carousel Mall)
This store is chock full of decorative and gift items. The walls are covered with art you can take home, and ornaments, jewelry, unusual clothing, and artistic pieces are everywhere.

LE GALERIE DOLLS AND MINIATURES
Market Street shopping tends to be more upscale than Main Street shopping, and Le Galerie leads the trend. The emphasis is on dolls, including Madame Alexander and Gene Schooley's native American dolls. The also have classic miniatures for doll houses, Christmas ornaments, and other unusual items.

LONDON SQUARE
Dwight LaPine and Jeff Shaffer, owners of London Square, draw your attention with their tasteful window displays and lead you through their store with their eclectic merchandise selection. You won't find traditional souvenirs here, but items that will always help you recall a Mackinac memory.

ENCHANTED GALLERY
Don't end your Market Street shopping before stopping into the Enchanted Gallery. Rob Jerstrom, the ultimate recorder of island scenes and events, has a gallery of his photographs that is not to be missed. He's mixed art items with his photographs to create a fascinating shop for the island lover.

These shops are on the side streets connecting Market and Main.

NADIA'S
A large upper-level clothing store for men and women, Nadia's is right in back of Doud's Mercantile on Fort Street. Nadia's carries a full line of sweaters, slacks, and shorts, and almost none of them have the Mackinac Island emblem.

BIRKENSTOCK
If you want to give your feet a treat, stop in at the Birkenstock store on Astor Street between Market and Main. This tiny store specializes in Birkenstock footwear and other foot friendly brands occasionally appear.

LOVE SHACK
With a name that intrigues, this store tends more to souvenirs than what you might imagine. Find it right next to the Birkenstock store.

THE GALLERY

The Gallery sells framed and unframed photography, watercolors, and pen and ink drawings of island and nature scenes. Look for it on Hoban Street right by the Village Inn.

GRAND HOTEL SHOPPING

Shoppers who are not guests of the hotel must pay a $7 admission fee to the hotel. To get to the Grand, take Main Street to Hoban, turn right on Hoban to Market, turn left on Market and bear right around Chamber's Riding Stable. You are now on Cadotte, which you follow up the hill to the Grand. The shops are all located on the lower level of the hotel.

MACKINAC MARKET

This is the best spot to buy Grand Hotel memorabilia, including robes, bags, glasses, sweatshirts, posters, and hats. The Market has a charming selection of children's games, toys, and books. It also has a nice gift book and music selection, and for those who want to pamper themselves or someone else, scented soaps and bath items are available.

MEDICINE MAN

Usually referred to as the newsstand, the Medicine Man is the Grand's answer to a typical hotel gift shop. In additional to the usual candy, cigarettes, and drug items, the Medicine Man has newspapers, magazines, paperbacks, and cards. It's also the only place you can buy specially bottled Grand Hotels wines and champagnes – perfect for reminding yourself of your island visit.

CARLETON'S TEA STORE

Named for Carleton Varney, the interior designer responsible for the Grand's good looks, Carleton's is a combination sandwich and tea shop and gift store. Carleton's has interesting cookbooks, homemade jams and jellies, teas and coffees, and unusual ceramics for the kitchen and dining room.

CAGNEY'S

Cagney's – For the Man of the World is a small upper-line clothing store for men. It carries the "after six" Grand Hotel essentials, including sport coats, ties, and bow ties, as well as some casual wear.

THE COLONY SHOP

The Colony Shop is a small upper-line clothing store for women, focusing primarily on fine casual and evening wear. It also carries costume jewelry, lingerie, purses, and hats.

T. RICHARD'S

Tucked into a back corner of the lower level, T. Richard's is a destination the young and young at heart won't forget. Located outside the arcade, T. Richard's has a wonderful collection of over 50 large glass canisters filled with treasures, candies, and trinkets. It also carries children's books, comic books, and coloring books.

OIL PAINTINGS BY MARLEE

Marlee grew up in northern Michigan and her oil paintings reflect a love of nature and of Mackinac Island, where she lives in the summer with her husband, Grand Hotel president Dan Musser III. Marlee's paintings grace the walls of many private and public collections, including the White House.

MARGARET'S GARDEN

If the Grand Hotel gardens inspire you, stop in at Margaret's Garden to take home some decorative accents for inside or outside your home. Vases, pillows, pots, watering cans, fountains, garden furniture, and gift items lean toward the whimsical and fun. Also a full-service florist, Margaret's Garden is named for one of the Musser granddaughters. Let them know if your name is Margaret; they have a surprise for you.

OTHER LOCATIONS

VISITOR'S CENTER
Primarily designed as an information storehouse, the Visitor's Center also has a wide selection of island and regional publications. The Visitor's Center is right across from Marquette Park.

SUTLER'S STORE
For unusual gifts and mementos with a historical bent, check out the Sutler's Store inside the walls of Fort Mackinac. Popular items include period musical instruments, military hats, coloring books with historical themes, and regional publications.

MACKINAC OUTFITTER & MARINE SUPPLY
Just east of the marina on the water, this is the ultimate shop for sailors and folks who like excellent gear. Classy sunglasses with famous names, foul weather clothing, and Patagonia jackets are all here. The other side of Hugh Ravitz's store gets practical and handles items to get yachters out of a jam.

BAY VIEW SHOP
Appealing to the boating crowd in the nearby marina, Bay View offers artifacts, gift items, and pictures with a nautical theme. There are ship clocks and lots of lighthouses, along with some nice clothing.

The Fudge Factor

Return from a visit to Mackinac Island without some fudge for your friends, and you'll be in big trouble. Mackinac is known as the land of fudge. Day visitors are called fudgies and fudge is the island's only exported product.

It all started in 1887 when the Murdick family saw the growth in Mackinac Island as a resort town and jumped on the opportunity. They started selling fudge to satisfy Victorian sweet tooths, and the tradition was born. Now there are 15 individual fudge shops on the island, owned by six different owners, producing more than 30 different flavors!

As you stroll down Main Street, you can't help but smell the fudge. The secret recipes are mixed in huge copper kettles, heated, and then poured onto marble slabs to begin the cooling process. Then a fudge flipper begins creaming the fudge by walking around the table, flipping the mixture with a long-handled spatula. They put on quite a show, keeping the fudge from hitting the floor. Finally, the fudge is worked into a loaf shape, and then sliced.

The fudge is sold for $9.95 a pound, and each slice is a half pound. The smallest amount you can buy at most stores is one-quarter pound. All of the fudge makers will provide free samples if you ask and will accept mail order requests between mid-May and mid-October.

Insiders stay away from naming a favorite fudge, so you'll have to sample and make your own decision (a very fun process in itself). To help you plan your taste-test, the chart on the next page provides the lowdown on locations, flavors, and policies of the fudge makers so you can make this very important decision. Most of the fudgemakers carry the standard flavors; selected special flavors are noted in the chart, but in this competitive business, these change frequently.

The standard fudge flavors include:
- chocolate
- chocolate nut
- chocolate peanut butter
- chocolate every other way
- rocky road
- maple
- maple pecan
- peanut butter
- vanilla
- vanilla nut
- rum walnut

Critical Fudge Facts

JoAnn's
Island Stores: 2
Special Flavors: Chocolate cherry, penuche, penuche pecan, raspberry truffle
Other Candies: Toffee, truffles, brittle, bark, caramel corn, stick candy
Notes: Many sugar free products

Kilwin's
Island Stores: 2
Special Flavors: Macadamia, raspberry walnut, orange cappuccino
Other Candies: Ice cream, lots of candies, caramel corn
Notes: Many sugar free products; mail order year-round

May's
Island Stores: 4
Special Flavors: Cherry
Other Candies: Pecan rolls, toffee, popcorn
Notes: 10% discount for seniors, scouts and islanders; does not accept
    credit cards; mail order year-round

Murdick's
Island Stores: 2
Special Flavors: Cranberry, chocolate macnut
Other Candies: Taffy, brittle, candies
Notes: Mail order year-round

Murray's
Island Stores: 1
Special Flavors: Amaretto, amaretto turtle, oreo coconut
Notes: Lowest priced fudge on the island; sold from Murray Hotel

Rena's
Island Stores: 1
Special Flavors: Cookie dough turtle, strawberry pecan
Other Candies: Taffy, some sugar-free candies, clusters, patties
Notes: Does not accept personal checks

Ryba's
Island Stores: 3
Special Flavors: Cookie dough turtle, strawberry pecan
Other Candies: Taffy, some sugar-free candies, clusters, patties
Notes: Does not accept personal checks; mail order year-round

8

Natural Attractions

As you approach Mackinac Island's harbor, vistas of high bluffs, deep blue waters, and luscious woods appear. You can begin to understand why Indians considered this land sacred and military leaders considered it a strategic post. The island's natural beauty and position in the middle of the Straits gave it historical significance. Ultimately, these same features helped secure its future as a tourist mecca.

This chapter reviews the island's natural attractions in general, describes many of the sights in detail, and wraps up with a suggested nature tour.

Remember when exploring the island not disturb its natural beauty. Taking pictures is fine; taking wildflowers is illegal.

The Island's Formation

Geologists say that Mackinac became an island about 15,000 years ago when the last glaciers receded from the area. The glaciers left a lake, later called "Algonquin." The highest part of the island, near what is now known as Fort Holmes, was the only portion visible above Lake Algonquin. The movement of Algonquin's waters created the island's bluffs and two of its limestone attractions, Skull Cave and Sugar Loaf.

About 9,000 years ago, Algonquin began to dry up. When it was at its lowest point, Mackinac Island and its nearby neighbors, Round Island and Bois Blanc Island, were connected to the mainland near the town of Cheboygan. Then the process reversed, and after another 4,000 years, one large lake called "Nippising" covered what are now Lakes Superior, Michigan, and Huron. Nippising's movements created more limestone formations, including Arch Rock, Friendship's Altar, and Eagle Point Cave. Over time, Nippising receded, leaving the three Great Lakes.

But the island's natural history has even deeper roots. The island's limestone formations began to form over 350 million years ago, when there was a thick layer of rock salt hundreds of feet below the area's limestone surface. As underground waters eroded the rock salt, large caverns were created underground. Over time, these collapsed, leaving stacks of broken limestone. Water gradually cemented these pieces together. Then Algonquin and Nippising washed away the softer rock around the stacks, leaving formations similar to what we see today. This type of formation, made of broken and re-cemented limestone, is called brecciated limestone, and is unique to northern Michigan.

"My favorite thing to do on Mackinac Island is to ride around the shore road, and to walk in the woods near Arch Rock and the Leslie Avenue area.

To get to know the island, you must spend more than a day, and see more than the downtown area. A carriage or bike tour is a good introduction, and then you should explore to really appreciate the beauty of the island. I think Mackinac Island's beauty and uniqueness stand out from any place in Michigan and perhaps the United States."

– Margaret Doud
Long-Serving Mackinac Island Mayor

Arch Rock is a spectacular natural bridge formation.

The Surrounding Waters

Mackinac Island sits in Lake Huron, near the Straits of Mackinac, which is a 50-mile passage connecting Lake Huron and Lake Michigan. Lake Huron has a surface area of 23,000 miles and is over 600 feet deep in some places. The Straits are an important shipping channel, with freighters carrying iron ore, coal, and lumber through the waters daily.

The area's waters are teeming with fish. The local favorite is whitefish, and you'll notice it on many of the island menus. Lake trout, once nearly depleted due to the invasion of parasitic sea lamprey, are again prevalent, thanks to a program of regulatory controls and restocking. Salmon are also becoming a favorite among sport fishermen.

' Living Things

Mackinac Island's unique weather and soil conditions put it in a transition zone for plant life between the softwood and evergreen (conifer) forests of the north and the mixed hardwoods of the south. The result is a bounty for nature lovers, with a wide variety of trees and wildflowers.

The island trees include the conifers (balsam, cedar, spruce, and tamarack) and the hardwoods (beech, black locust, red oak, and sugar maple). The

South Bicycle Trail is an excellent place to view the varieties, as they are well marked along this route.

The island's wildflowers number over 400 species, spread throughout a range of habitats. Walk slowly along any of the island trails and you are sure to be pleased by the delicate carpets of wildflowers.

Along the beaches, look for beach pea, wrinkled rose, silverweed, and sedum. In the bogs, look for blueberries, heath, and wild orchids. The marshes feature marsh marigold, March blue violet, cattails, and mints. In the meadows seek out daisies, wild strawberries, blue-eyed grass, and campions. In the softwood forests, look for bead lily, calypso orchid, and twin flower. In the hardwood forests, search for trillium, mayflower, and trout lily.

The island wildlife is not as varied as its plant life. Mackinac's year-round bird population is primarily purple finch, red-breasted nuthatch, and black-capped chickadee. The summer population swells with the addition of hummingbirds, sea gulls, robins, yellow warblers, chimney swifts, American redstart, ovenbirds, and a variety of swallows. The most prominent mammals are squirrels, bats, raccoons, chipmunks, and rabbits.

Sights to See

ANNE'S TABLET

An almost secret hideaway visited mostly by locals, Anne's Tablet sits high on a bluff above the Indian Dormitory and Marquette Park. The large stone tablet and several stone benches are surrounded by hills of myrtle. Anne's Tablet is dedicated to Constance Fenimore Woolson, an author who wrote the book *Anne* in the late 1800's. This spot is great for quiet reflection or a picnic for two, with a marvelous view of the harbor. Take Crow's Nest Trail behind the playground at Marquette Park. When you reach the top, take the trail to your immediate left, before the East Bluff road.

ARCH ROCK

Located on the island's eastern shore, Arch Rock is the most spectacular of the island's brecciated limestone formations. The limestone arch rises 146 feet above the water and spans 50 feet. A stairway from the shore road leads to the top of the arch.

Indian legend says the arch was formed when an Indian maiden, forbidden by her father to marry the warrior of her dreams, cried for so long that her tears washed away the bluff's stone and created the arch. The sad story has a happy ending; the warrior appears and takes the maiden with him to his home among the sky people. The Indians also believed that Arch Rock was where the Great Spirit entered the island before taking up residence in Sugar Loaf, the great wigwam.

A sacred place for early Native Americans,
Sugar Loaf continues to amaze visitors.

SUGAR LOAF

Sugar Loaf, the largest of the island's limestone stacks, towers 75 feet above the ground. Lake Algonquin once covered Sugar Loaf up to the point of the small cave on the stack's north side. You can find Sugar Loaf by following Sugar Loaf Road in the island's interior.

SKULL CAVE

Skull Cave is one of the island's oldest formations, and has an interesting history. The cave was formed as Lake Algonquin's waves washed against a large limestone stack and eroded a portion of its western side, leaving a cave. The cave was apparently used as an Indian burial ground, as Alexander Henry, a British merchant, discovered. He hid there one night after the Indians took Fort Michilimackinac on the mainland in 1763, and discovered the bones when he awoke. Since it was a sacred site to the Indians, they did not pursue him within the cave and his life was spared. Skull Cave is at the intersection of Garrison and Rifle Range Roads.

CAVE IN THE WOODS

Cave in the Woods is a small cave located near the island's airport. It was created about 10,000 years ago, when the location was a beach of Lake Algonquin.

Some of the island's lilac trees are over 300 years old.

CRACK IN THE ISLAND

A long, shallow fissure in the surface limestone, Crack in the Island is located near Cave in the Woods. The Crack was formed in much the same way as the limestone formations. Water eroded the softer rock and left brecciated limestone.

DEVIL'S KITCHEN

Located on Mackinac's western shore right by the shore road, Devil's Kitchen is one of the youngest limestone formations on the island. Although the limestone has been in place for 350 million years, the erosion forming the small cave has taken place in the last few centuries.

BROWN'S BROOK

A beautiful spot between town and British Landing, Brown's Brook is surrounded by cedar trees and nice big rocks to take a rest from a bike ride. It is fed by an underground spring and flows year round.

CROGHAN'S WATER

Croghan's Water is a seasonal marsh near British Landing. In the spring, it is an excellent spot to see vegetation and animals. It is named after Colonel Croghan who led the Americans in an ill-fated attempt to regain Fort Mackinac from the British in July of 1814.

Natural Attractions Bike Tour

Mackinac's natural beauty surrounds you when you visit. But if you are really interested in seeing the sights just described, you need to go up in the middle of the island. This tour gets you to most of the more impressive natural sites. Because of the distances involved, you will need to travel on a bicycle. The tour is fairly rigorous, and takes about three hours.

Beginning at Marquette Park, find Fort Street on the western edge of the park, and push your bike up the hill, through the brown gates, to the top. You will be beside the Governor's summer residence at that point. Turn right to go past Fort Mackinac. Go across the main intersection and pick up the South Bicycle Trail. Take it to Arch Rock.

After viewing Arch Rock, take Rifle Range Road (to your right when your back is to Arch Rock) to its end, and turn right on Garrison Road. Explore Skull Cave, then take Garrison Road past the cemeteries, and turn right on Fort Holmes Road. To your left is a hardwood forest. Stay to the right, and go up to Fort Holmes (the highest point on the island) for a fantastic view of the entire Straits area. Congratulate yourself, because it's all downhill from Fort Holmes. On the way down, bear to the right and look out over Sugar Loaf. Take Fort Holmes Road back to Garrison Road and turn right.

Follow Garrison past the end of the air strip and past the intersection of four roads, where Garrison turns into British Landing Road, and turn left on State Road. Park, and hike on the trail to your left to examine Cave of the Woods and Crack in the Island.

Take State Road back to British Landing Road and turn left. Take British Landing Road past the battlefield meadow on the right and the marshes of Croghan's Water. Stop in at the nature center at British Landing to ask any questions you may have.

Right or left on the shore road will take you back to town. Left is shorter and takes you past Brown's Brook, which is a nice spot to rest. If you go right, you can stop at the Wild Flower Trail and view Arch Rock from the shore.

9

Historical Treasures

The Straits area is a history-lover's delight. Along these picturesque shores, Indians, French Jesuits, French voyageurs, British fur traders, and American soldiers lived, worked, and played. Later, Victorian travelers discovered the island and its special magic. Through the efforts of the Mackinac State Historic Parks; the City of Mackinac Island; and the Chambers of Commerce of Mackinac Island, Mackinaw City and St. Ignace, this rich history comes alive for the inquisitive modern-day visitor.

The best way to learn about the island's history is to visit the historical attractions, view the displays, and talk to the well-informed guides. Then wander through the attractions and picture for yourself what has transpired on this little island over the past 300 years.

To help set the stage for your exploration, a "short course" in island history follows, and then each attraction is described in detail. At the end of the chapter, I'll recommend three tours routes to take on your historical exploration and some side trips to historical treasures in the Straits areas near the island.

A Short Course in Mackinac Island History

The first records of Mackinac Island history are found in Indian lore, which says the island appeared one day out of a deep fog that had clouded the Straits for several days. The Indian meaning of the name is still disputed, but most accounts indicate that Michilimackinac (later shortened to Mackinac) means "great turtle," and is a reference to the island's shape. The other theory is that the Indian name for the island was actually Mishi-min-auk-in-ong, which means a place of the great dancing spirits. Indians believed that the Great Spirit came to the island to live among his people in the large limestone wigwam (Sugar Loaf). The island served as a sacred land for many Indians, and they offered gifts to the spirits on the island and buried their dead here.

Almost all of the Indians in the area were descendants of the Algonquin, Iroquois, or Sioux tribes. The tribes frequently had conflicts among themselves, but the arrival of the French intensified the struggle. The land was rich with natural resources and, for the Indians, it was sacred. For the non-Indians, it represented a strategic location.

"Mackinac Island is such a special place because it combines a beautiful and unusual natural setting with over three hundred years of recorded history. The one hundred year old ban on automobiles helps the island retain its historic ambience. The presence of nearly five hundred horses and the sights, sounds, and smells of an earlier time help the visitor to enjoy the island at a more relaxed pace.

If possible, visitors should stay overnight. It's a special treat to walk around in the long summer evenings enjoying the tranquility and beauty of the island."

— ***David Armour***
Mackinac State Historic Parks

Father Marquette was a key figure in the area's history.

The first non-Indian reported to have traveled through the Straits was Jean Nicolet. Nicolet was a French explorer en route from Quebec to what he believed was China in 1664 when he traveled through the Straits, discovered Wisconsin, and almost reached the Mississippi River. In 1669, Father Jean Claude Allouez, a French Jesuit, visited the island from his mission at Sault Ste. Marie. That same year, Father Claude Dablon built a bark chapel on the island to help spread Christianity among Indians of the Straits area. Because of the isolation of the island in the winter, Dablon decided to re-establish the mission on the mainland near what is now St. Ignace, and directed Father Jacques Marquette to lead this mission.

Meanwhile, interest was building among the French to explore what Nicolet had called the "Great Water." (This turned out to be the Mississippi River, but he thought it was the ocean.) Louis Joliet and Father Marquette were sent in 1674 to find the Great Water, and they did.

The Jesuits were great explorers, but their amicable relationships with the Indians were increasingly at odds with French economic and military desires. The importance of spreading Christianity became secondary to the importance of expanding the fur trade. The Jesuits received less support, and by the mid-1700s had little influence in the area.

Fur pelts were rapidly becoming the currency of the day, and the French wanted to establish a series of fur trading posts, linked with forts, throughout the Great Lakes. Toward this end, they built Fort de Baude in 1690 in St. Ignace near the Jesuit mission. This fort operated for about 10 years before it was ordered closed and the mission moved to Fort Pontchartrain (Detroit).

The French move opened the way for the British to establish a presence in the Straits. When the French realized their mistake, they returned to the area, and in 1715 constructed Fort Michilimackinac (Mackinaw City). In the ensuing years, the French and the British continued to skirmish. When the skirmishes turned to war, the British won Canada, which encompassed much of the Midwest, including Michigan.

The British did not cultivate relationships with the Indians as the French had, and consequently had disastrous results. In 1763, what looked like an Indian ball game outside the walls of Fort Michilimackinac turned into the Indian capture of the Fort and a massacre of the British soldiers. Fearing British retaliation, the Indians moved to a more defensible position on Mackinac Island. When they didn't get the support they expected from the French, the Indians ended their stand, and the British moved back to Fort Michilimackinac within the year. But the British had learned the value of good relationships with the local Indian tribes.

When the British at Michilimackinac learned of the American Revolution, they decided, as the Indians had in 1763, that they should move to a more defensible position on Mackinac Island. Major Patrick Sinclair and his troops began moving buildings and supplies across the ice in the winter of 1779. By the following summer, the move was complete. A fortress was built on the bluff overlooking the harbor, while settlers and traders built homes along the shore. Despite continued rumors that the Americans were going to attack the fort, there were no British-American battles at the Straits during the Revolution. The area was transferred to the Americans in the Treaty of Paris in 1783, but the British managed to delay turning Fort Mackinac over to the Americans in 1796.

In the early 1800's, the Americans worked to establish dominance in the fur trade, but their plans were upset in 1812 when the U.S. Government declared war against the British. The new government's communication system was poor, and the Americans on Mackinac Island did not learn of the war until the British secretly landed on the back of the island (British Landing), hauled a cannon up to its highest point, and pointed it down on Fort Mackinac. The Americans surrendered without a shot being fired, and the British were back in command.

The Americans tried to recapture the island in 1814, using the strategy of approaching Fort Mackinac from the back of the island, but the British were prepared. After a bloody battle, the Americans retreated. Not long afterward, the Americans attempted a naval blockade of the island, but that failed too.

Mackinac Island was returned to the Americans through the Treaty of Ghent, signed in 1814. Because the U.S. Government prohibited British companies from doing business in the United States, Americans quickly took over the fur trading industry. John Jacob Astor consolidated his hold, setting up headquarters of his American Fur Trading Company on Mackinac Island. In time, he became extremely prosperous and was one of the country's first millionaires. Fur trading remained the dominant force on the island until the 1840s when a decline in demand and a reduced availability of pelts combined to seriously hurt the business.

The decline in the fur trade caused Mackinac Island merchants to look for a new industry. They realized what the Indians had known for years: the Straits were filled with fish. The island quickly transformed from a fur trading center to a base for fishing fleets.

Many of the early summer residents were from Chicago.

Fishing shanties, processing shops, and related businesses popped up on Main Street. Several docks were built. The fishermen used nets to catch the fish, and then brought them to Mackinac Island to be processed and shipped by steamship to Detroit, Chicago, and other major markets. Mackinac Island's economy was dependent on fishing for about 40 years, until a combination of over-fishing and increased tourism caused another dramatic shift in the island's industry in about 1880.

The Arnold Line dock was as busy in 1910 as it is today,
and much more orderly!

At that time, the steamship and railroad companies were looking for passengers, and began to promote Mackinac Island as an idyllic summer getaway for upper-middle-class Midwesterners. The industrialization of America was creating a leisure class that wanted to escape the heat and pollution of the cities in summer. They expected to travel in luxury, and the steamship and railroad companies were happy to oblige.

In 1875, Congress had named Mackinac Island the nation's second national park (Yellowstone was the first), securing its future as a tourist destination. The first railroad reached Mackinaw City in 1881, and regular ferry service to the island began that same year. The island put on a new set of clothes, changing out of its fishing garb into a wardrobe a Victorian socialite would enjoy. Fashionable shops were established, excellent restaurants opened, and increasingly sophisticated hotels catered to the new visitors. Travelers would arrive on the docks accompanied by maids and servants, and equipped with trunks filled with elaborate clothing for the events of the day: formal meals, teas, and dances. Many would stay the entire summer.

Demand quickly grew for private cottages. Gordon Hubbard, who had worked for the American Fur Trading Company and then made and lost a fortune in Chicago, decided to develop his 80 acres of land on the island. He sold his first lots in 1882, and Charles Caskey, a builder from Harbor Springs, quickly built several cottages in Hubbard's Annex. The design was simple in those original Caskey cottages, and a few unadorned ones remain today. Most of them were expanded extensively as the island gained favor as a resort.

The national park began leasing land to prospective cottage owners, and building began to take place on the island's eastern and western bluffs. Proceeds from the leases were used to improve the park properties.

By 1887, a consortium of railroad and steamship companies hired Charles Caskey to build a magnificent hotel on Mackinac Island. It was a gamble designed to increase demand for the trains and ships giving service to the island. The original portion of the Grand Hotel was built in four months, almost exclusively of Michigan white pine. It was a struggle to keep the 200 rooms full, and the short season made it difficult to break even.

By the turn of the century, thanks to aggressive promotional activity, the Grand Hotel was a success. With an elegant hotel and a socialite cottage scene, Mackinac Island became a truly grand resort town.

Two other key decisions were made at this time that improved Mackinac's position as a resort. In 1895, the U.S. Government transferred its properties on the island to the state of Michigan, making it the state's first state park. This move ensured that the island would be protected from developers seeking to expand the residential and commercial building on the island. And in 1896, the first actions were taken to prohibit motor vehicles from operating on the island.

Throughout the 1900s, the island solidified its position as a major destination for travelers in the Midwest. More hotels and businesses opened, and the state began to improve its land and facilities as tourist attractions. In the 1920s, the state doubled the size of the park, and eventually over 80 percent of the island's land became state park. The old fort pasture was turned into Marquette Park, and other historical buildings were acquired by the state.

The island weathered the Depression and two world wars fairly well. Tourism received another boost when the Mackinac Bridge was completed in 1957, connecting Michigan's Upper and Lower Peninsulas. Not long afterwards, the state began an aggressive program of excavation and renovation beginning with Fort Mackinac.

College students in military costume fire cannons from Fort Mackinac daily.

Overview of Historical Attractions

Before setting out on a historical tour, read the attraction descriptions below and decide which ones you want to see. Some suggested routes are outlined at the end of the chapter, but your interests will determine the best route for you.

Most of the attractions require a ticket (the Historic Mackinac Island Ticket), which you can purchase at the Visitor's Center across the street from Marquette Park. The Visitor's Center has informative displays and staff on hand who can explain the various ticket options and answer many of your questions.

INDIAN DORMITORY

Just east of Marquette Park, the Indian Dormitory looks more like an outpost of Fort Mackinac than a dormitory built for Indians. Built in 1838, the Indian Dormitory never really worked for its original purpose, which was to house Indian chieftains when they came to the island to exchange goods with soldiers and townspeople.

The Indian Dormitory is the best place on the island to get a sense of Native American history. It contains a wealth of information about Henry Schoolcraft, the Indian agent in the 1830's who studied the Indians in great detail. It includes artifacts and dioramas arranged along the theme of Henry Wadsworth Longfellow's classic poem, *Hiawatha*. Longfellow was a friend of Schoolcraft's, and based his poem on Schoolcraft's works. Admission is by Historic Mackinac Island Ticket.

FORT MACKINAC

Located on the bluff high above the harbor, Fort Mackinac is a must for visitors. There are two entrances, and both involve a pretty hefty climb. The front ramp is visible from Marquette Park. The second entrance is reached by taking Fort Street up through the brown wooden gates, and up the hill to the Governor's summer residence. Bear right to reach the entrance to the Fort at the Avenue of Flags. If you want to avoid the climb, see the Fort at the end of a carriage tour. Drivers stop at the Avenue of Flags and let tour participants disembark there.

You'll immediately see why the British chose this site, with its commanding view of the Straits, for their fort. Start your tour with the short slide presentation shown regularly in the Commissary Building near the main entrance. After that, tour the buildings in any order you like; you'll find that each has a self-contained story, and that many interpreters are available to answer your questions. By the time the guides announce their Parade Ground show, with interpretation and musket firings, you'll have great insight into how the soldiers lived, fought, got sick, and entertained themselves in this island post. Admission is by the Historic Mackinac Ticket.

BRITISH LANDING

British Landing is on the back side of the island, and not surprisingly, this is where the British landed in 1812 to launch their sneak attack on the Americans at Fort Mackinac. There is a nature center just off the beach. A crowd always forms here, because it is a good resting place for bike riders going the distance around the island. A snack shop and public rest rooms are available.

BATTLEFIELD OF 1814

Up British Landing Road from British Landing is the Battlefield of 1814. This time it was the Americans landing in an attempt to regain possession of Fort Mackinac. After a bloody battle on this site, the Americans retreated, and eventually secured the Fort by treaty.

FORT HOLMES

A visit to Fort Holmes on the island's highest point requires some energetic climbing, by foot or bicycle, but the view is worth the effort. This is where the British set up their cannon in 1812 and took Fort Mackinac from the Americans without a shot being fired. The site was later fortified with a small stockade and blockhouse. Only a reconstructed stockade remains on this site, which is 168 feet above Fort Mackinac and 325 feet above the Straits.

GOVERNOR'S SUMMER RESIDENCE

This lovely home, just west of Fort Mackinac, is owned by the state of Michigan. It was built in 1902 for a prominent Chicago attorney at a cost of $15,000. By 1945, the 24-room home had fallen on hard times, and it was purchased by the state for its building cost. It has served as a summer home for Michigan's Governor ever since.

Lots of conferences are centered here throughout the season, and political dignitaries are entertained. To join in the fun, ask at the Visitor's Center about touring the first floor of the home. Recent governors have allowed the public to tour one day per week. If you walk by the home, enjoy the gardens visible over the fence, and look at the gazebo in the yard which was built for the movie, *Somewhere In Time*.

As you might imagine, Michigan governors develop a love for the island during their term in office. Former governors G. Mennen Williams and William Milliken moved into their own island homes after leaving office.

MISSIONARY BARK CHAPEL

The Bark Chapel in Marquette Park depicts the type of worshipping place constructed by Father Claude Dablon in 1669. There is a peacefulness in this tiny chapel, and a depiction of Father Dablon's mission.

TRINITY EPISCOPAL CHURCH

Across from the Bark Chapel is Trinity Episcopal Church, which was built in 1882. Episcopalian services were held on the island beginning in 1842. The church is picturesque, full of banners and wood, and has a large summer congregation. President Ford attended services here during his visit as President.

LITTLE STONE CHURCH

Located at the bottom of the Grand Hill is the Little Stone Congregational Church, with its stained glass windows depicting scenes from the island's history. The congregation was formed mainly by cottage-owners, and their personal contributions led to the construction of this unique church, which was completed in 1904. The building is open to the public in the summer when it is not being used for services or weddings.

ST. ANNE'S CATHOLIC CHURCH

St. Anne's is located two blocks east of Marquette Park. Although the current building was built in 1878, the Catholic roots of St. Anne's go back to Father Dablon in the mid-1600s. The first St. Anne's church was within the walls of Fort Michilimackinac, and it was one of the first buildings moved across the ice to the island when the British moved Fort Mackinac in 1779.

There is a museum in the basement of the church that includes records, articles, and paintings from the original church. Large private donations recently saved St. Anne's from near-disaster when sections of the bell tower and the building were deteriorating. A large church hall was added recently, and it is the center of winter activity among residents.

St. Anne's has a legacy of colorful priests who become a mainstay for the resident population. In the wintertime, people of all faiths meet together at St. Anne's.

MISSION CHURCH

Mission Church, located on Huron Street just west of Mission Point Resort, is the oldest surviving church building in Michigan. It was built in 1829, in New England style architecture. During a recent renovation effort, a campaign was launched to Adopt-a-Pew, and the original high-backed pews with doors were saved by generous donations. The church is now a popular spot for weddings, but no public services take place here.

Market Street Historical Attractions

McGULPIN HOUSE

McGulpin House is one of the oldest structures on the island, dating back to the 1780s. Located near the corner of Market and Fort Streets, it has been restored and includes an exhibit showing the construction techniques of the time. Admission is by the Historic Mackinac Ticket.

BEAUMONT MEMORIAL

Another attraction with admission by the Historic Mackinac Ticket, the Beaumont Memorial is located on the corner of Market and Fort streets. It is a tribute to Dr. William Beaumont, an Army physician during the Fort's occupation by American troops.

In 1882, Alexis St. Martin, a young Frenchman shopping in the American Fur Trading Company store, was shot in the stomach. The Fort physician, Dr. Beaumont, treated him but the hole in his stomach did not heal. This freak accident allowed Dr. Beaumont to research the human digestive system. He lowered foods into St. Martin's stomach through the hole and watched digestion at work. This incident and the significant repercussions are shown in exhibits in the Beaumont Memorial. As in all of the state park attractions, costumed guides are on hand to answer questions.

ROBERT STUART HOUSE

The Stuart House on Market Street is a museum operated by the City of Mackinac Island. Always an interesting spot to visit, the museum has undergone renovation and is an improved version of the home occupied from 1817-1837 by the manager of the American Fur Company. In the

1840s, it served as the island's first hotel. It is chock full of antiques, old photographs, artifacts and sketches of the early families on Mackinac Island. Take your time wandering through the Stuart House. There's a lot of interesting history here. A nominal admission charge applies.

AMERICAN FUR COMPANY WAREHOUSE

Next to the Robert Stuart House, the American Fur Company Warehouse is where pelts were sorted, graded, cleaned, and pressed for shipment to the east coast. It was built in 1810, and is now owned by the City of Mackinac Island. A recent federal grant enabled the City to redo the building from its internals outward, replacing rotted timbers and putting a new face on the warehouse. Now it serves as a Community Hall, giving local residents a gathering and meeting place.

COUNTY COURT HOUSE

From 1834, when it was built, until 1882, the next building served as the county courthouse. Now it houses the police, jail, and city council chambers.

Built in the 1890s, this cottage on the West Bluff is an example of Queen Anne artchitecture.

EDWARD BIDDLE HOUSE

The Edward Biddle House is one of the oldest structures downtown, originally built as early as 1780. It is restored and furnished as it was when Edward Biddle, a prominent fur trader, and his Indian wife lived there. Interpreters demonstrate wool spinning and baking. Admission is by Historic Mackinac Ticket.

BENJAMIN BLACKSMITH SHOP

Behind the Biddle House, the Benjamin Blacksmith Shop is a working museum that is guaranteed to delight the children in the crowd. Watch the smithy continue in the tradition of long-time island blacksmith Herbert Benjamin as he coaxes iron into the shape of wagon rims, street light brackets, and candle holders. Many of these handmade items are available for sale to the public. Admission is by Historic Mackinac Ticket.

Suggested Historical Routes

Decide which historical sights you want to see and plot your own tour, or pick one of these to follow:

EARLY INDIAN AND MILITARY HISTORY
(about 2½ hours)
Begin at Marquette Park, after purchasing the Historic Mackinac Ticket at the Visitor's Center. Explore the Bark Chapel, and stop to admire Father Marquette's statue and his frequent bird friends that perch on the top of his head. Wander over to the Indian Dormitory to learn more about Indian life. On your way up the hill to Fort Mackinac, stop at the McGulpin House to see how early settlers lived. Huff and puff up to the Fort (it's okay, everyone does), and learn firsthand about the military history. Exit the Fort at the Avenue of Flags, turn left and see the Governor's summer residence straight ahead. Bear left at the Governor's and return to Marquette Park.

FUR TRADERS, TOURISTS, AND VICTORIAN COTTAGES
(about 3 hours)
Purchase a Historic Mackinac Ticket at the Visitor's Center. Walk past the Bark Chapel in Marquette Park and across to Market Street. Explore the Beaumont Memorial on the corner, and then wander down the full length of Market Street visiting museums that will acquaint you with Beaumont, Astor, Stuart, Biddle, and Benjamin. Continue on Market Street until you reach the Chamber's Riding Stable and turn right to go up the

Grand Hill. There is an admission fee to enter the hotel, but the grandeur of the Victorian Age is alive and well here. If you have the buffet lunch, they credit you with a portion of the admission fee.

Coming off the Grand porch, continue to the right and walk up the beautiful West Bluff. The cottages are largely in Queen Anne style Victorian, and were built after the national park began to lease land in the late 1800s. The fourth cottage from the Grand Hotel is the one previously owned by G. Mennen Williams, former Governor of Michigan.

At the end of the West Bluff the paved road turns to the right and then to the left. Make this jog, then stay to the left at the next intersection. Follow this road until you reach the large, white-columned Greek Revival home on your left. Turn right and go through Hubbard's Annex, the home of many fine cottages. Many of these places were initially constructed by Charles Caskey, then expanded and ornamented to become the stately Victorians they are today.

To return to Marquette Park, turn right on Annex Road and go back to Grand Hill, past the hotel and back into town. You might want to take a right turn at the bottom of the hill and go to the shore road and turn left. Many of the homes along this shoreline were purchased by cottagers and have become summer homes. This is also the location of the boardwalk and the library.

Fort Michilimackinac is on the shore, next to the Mackinac Bridge.

FORTS AND BATTLEFIELDS
(about 2 hours, plus time to visit Fort Mackinac)
Bicycles are recommended for this tour, which will take you past the island's forts and battlefields. Beginning at Marquette Park, push your bike up the street bordering the park (Fort Street), and through the brown gates to the Governor's summer residence. Turn right and ride to the fort for a short or a long visit. Come back out the Avenue of Flags, grab your bike and continue on the road to your right to Garrison, in front of the Boy Scout barracks. Take a left to go past Skull Cave and the historic cemeteries.

After the second cemetery on your right, turn right and you will be on your way to Fort Holmes. Bear to the right as you go up. A word of warning: the carriage tours used to bring groups to Fort Holmes, but it was discontinued because it was such a tough climb for the horses. On the way back down from Fort Holmes, bear to your right and look out over Sugar Loaf below.

When you get back to the cemeteries, turn right on Garrison Road. This turns into British Landing Road at the main intersection. Follow British Landing Road past the Battlefield of 1814 and Croghan's Water, and down the hill to the shore. From British Landing, the shore road to the left goes back to town the short way.

Related Historical Outings

FORT MICHILIMACKINAC, 616/436-5563

Fort Michilimackinac in Mackinaw City is a reconstruction of the fur-trading village and fort established in 1715 by the French on that site. There are ongoing archaeological digs, craft demonstrations, costumed interpreters, and displays for visitors to enjoy. There is also a maritime museum inside the restored 1892 Mackinac Point Lighthouse on the site. Admission fee applies; if you plan to visit both Fort Mackinac and Fort Michilimackinac, ask about a combination ticket at either fort or at the Visitor's Center on Mackinac Island.

MACKINAC BRIDGE MUSEUM, 616/436-5534

A former ironworker developed this museum above his pizzeria in Mackinaw City to recognize the people who built the Mackinac Bridge. It contains interesting tools and artifacts, and a continuously running film about the bridge's construction. Admission is free. The museum is located above Mama Mia's Pizza in Mackinaw City.

OLD MILL CREEK, 616/436-7301

Old Mill Creek is a 625-acre park on U.S. 23 just outside Mackinaw City. Its main attraction is a working reconstructed eighteenth century watermill. Enjoy craft demonstrations, nature trails, a multi-media orientation program, and a picnic area. There is a nominal admission fee or admission through the fort combination ticket.

MUSEUM OF OJIBWA CULTURE, 906/643-9161

This museum in downtown St. Ignace tells the story of the Ojibwa (also known as Chippewa) life in the Straits area. It is built on the site of the Father Marquette mission, and archaeological digs continue to uncover artifacts from that era. Nominal admission fee.

SAULT STE. MARIE BOAT LOCKS

The "Soo" is one of Michigan's oldest cities and home to the Soo locks, connecting Lakes Superior and Huron. It is a 55-mile drive from St. Ignace. For additional information, contact:

Sault Area Chamber of Commerce
2581 I-75 Business Spur
Sault Ste. Marie, MI 49783
906/632-3301
www.saultstemarie.com.

10

Good Sports

With clean air and beautiful scenery, Mackinac Island is a natural for the sports enthusiast. The options are many and, in most cases, the cost is minimal.

The suggested routes for bicycling, hiking, and jogging described below are designed for both exercising and sightseeing. They are organized from easiest to most difficult by category. Starting off with no route in mind is just fine, too. If you get lost, remember you are on an island and you can always find the water, follow it, and get back to town. The directions contained here have landmarks as well as road names, since signage is relatively new to the island.

BICYCLING

Bicycles are an excellent way to explore the island while getting exercise. Bike rental facts and related information appears in Chapter Five.

Round the Rock *(The most level eight miles of ground you'll find on the island).* This is the most popular biking route on the island. Take the shore road from town in either direction and enjoy fewer people, a level paved road, and lovely views of the water and woods. You may want to stop at Devil's Kitchen, British Landing, the Wild Flower Trail, or Arch Rock along the way.

South BicycleTrail Saunter *(Approximately four miles on paved roads with one long uphill stretch).* From Marquette Park, take the shore road east away from downtown. After you pass Haan's 1830 Inn, take a left on the first road leading up the hill. Ride or push your bike up Mission Hill (most push!). Stay to the left at the top of the hill and take Huron Street past the East Bluff cottages.

Turn right on the South Bicycle Trail, which is after you pass the East Bluff cottages and at the intersection of three paved roads (it's marked with a bicycle sign). Follow the South Bicycle Trail to Arch Rock. Then take Rifle Range Road, which is to the right when your back is to Arch Rock. Turn right on Sugar Loaf Road, which loops past this limestone formation and ends back at Rifle Range Road. Take a right and follow Rifle Range Road until you get to Garrison Road. Turn left. Then turn right on Huron (the first road to the right) and go past the Fort. Bear left on Fort Street at the Governor's summer residence, then walk your bike down the hill back to Marquette Park.

North Bicycle Trail Trek *(Approximately six miles, fairly hilly, mostly paved).* From Marquette Park, push your bike between the brown gates and up the Fort Street hill. Go past the Governor's summer residence, turn right, and go past Fort Mackinac. Turn left on Garrison Road just past the Boy Scout barracks, and go past the South Bicycle Trail. Take a right on the North Bicycle Trail. As you approach a large paved road (Rifle Range) veer left on a short path, cross Rifle Range, and continue on the wide asphalt and dirt path.

Pass Sugar Loaf on the right and the stairs to Point Lookout on the left, and continue on the North Bicycle Trail until it ends at Leslie Avenue. Turn left down the hill onto Leslie, take it to where it ends at British Landing Road and turn left. Go past the end of the airport and turn right on Annex Road. Turn right again on Stonecliffe Road. Checkout the Stonecliffe

Resort and restaurants, and then take Stonecliffe Road back to Annex Road and turn right. Follow Annex Road past the cottages on your right. Turn right and go down the hill past the Grand Hotel. Turn left at the Chamber's Riding Stable and take Market Street back to Marquette Park.

BOATING

If floating on the water instead of staring at it from the shore is your thing, contact Captain Harold DeHart to arrange a private cruise. He'll do weddings on the water, sunset and sunrise cruises, or whatever you want. Rates are about $30 per person per hour, with a minimum of $120 per hour. Captain DeHart can be reached on his boat in season at 906/847-6580 or 888/847-6580. In the off season, call him at 517/733-8569.

FISHING

The Straits are an excellent place to catch king, coho and kokanee salmon, brown and lake trout, and steelheads. Because the water is so shallow near the shore, and there is so much activity in the harbor, fishing off the shore or the boat docks is not recommended.

Charter companies will arrange half or full day fishing trips and provide all the equipment. For more information, contact Captain Harold DeHart for a referral (see above).

FREIGHTER WATCHING

Freighter watching is an art form on Mackinac Island. Summer residents track the comings and goings of their favorite freighters and know when to expect them to pass through the Straits. They pride themselves on being able to name the freighters without using binoculars.

A quick primer: boats headed west are usually down-bound and loaded with iron ore from the Minnesota area. They have passed through Lake Superior, the Sault Ste. Marie boat locks, and upper Lake Huron. As they pass the island they are headed for Lake Michigan, Chicago and Gary, Indiana. The usually return empty in three or four days.

Occasionally a freighter from some foreign port goes by. Called "salties" by insiders because they are ocean-going vessels, these freighters are distinguished by a shorter length and two superstructures, fore and aft.

Pick up a freighter-watching guide at the local bookstore and keep track of sightings during your visit.

GOLF

There are three golf courses on Mackinac Island offering very different experiences for golfers. Pick your favorite or try them all.

The Jewel. Located adjacent to the Grand Hotel, the Jewel is a well-maintained nine-hole course that is popular with hotel guests and local residents. Electric carts, pull carts, and clubs can all be rented. There is a small pro shop on the grounds. Call 906/847-3331 to arrange a tee time and inquire about rates.

The Woods. Developed by the Grand Hotel so its guests could play 18 holes, the Woods has quickly become a favorite spot to play a round of nine holes as well. For a unique day of golf, the two courses can be played as 18 with a horse-drawn golf carriage ride between holes 9 and 10. Call 906/847-3331 to arrange tee times and inquire about rates.

Wawashkamo. This nine-hole course was created by summer cottagers at the turn of the century and is one of the few traditional Scottish Links courses in the country. The golfer who enjoys golf in the rough loves to play Wawashkamo, and can use the same nine to play back for 18 holes.

The club house is a charming structure, just what you would imagine for a Victorian society membership. Now the course is open to the public, although the membership is still thriving with social events and tournaments. Electric carts, pull carts, and clubs can be rented. Call 906/847-3871 to arrange a tee time and inquire about rates.

HIKING

The possibilities for a wonderful hike are endless. Head off with a good map and a sense of adventure or try one of my favorites:

Woodsy Walk *(about two hours on a mix of trails and roads)*. Start at the back of Marquette Park behind the playground by the Indian Dormitory. Take Crow's Nest Trail up the hill. Turn right on Huron Road and go past the East Bluff cottages. When you reach the fork in the road at Mission Hill, stay to the left and continue past more cottages. Watch for Winnebago Trail on your left and take it to the end.

Go across the paved road and pick up Rock Trail, a small path that goes to the left. Turn right from Rock Trail onto Lime Kiln Trail. Take Lime Kiln until it ends at the North Bicycle Trail, which is paved, and turn right. After a short distance turn left on the paved Rifle Range Road. Watch for a stairway on the right. For extra credit, scamper up it and you'll find Fort Holmes.

There are over 50 marked trails throughout the island.

Rest and enjoy the view, then follow the road that says Point Lookout past the water station and bear right. Look at the view of Sugar Loaf from Point Lookout, then continue down the hill and turn left on Garrison Road. At the intersection of three roads, stay to the left and pass the cemeteries.

At Skull Cave, bear right. At another intersection of three roads, turn right on Huron Road and go past Fort Mackinac. At the Governor's summer residence, turn left, and take Fort Street down the hill to Marquette Park.

Eastern Experience *(3 to 4 hours on some challenging trails; not recommended with small children).* From Marquette Park take the shore road east away from downtown. Turn left on the first side street, Bogan Lane, which is just past the "painted lady" called the Inn on Mackinac. Take the stairs at the end of Bogan Lane up the bluff and turn right. Go past the East Bluff cottages and at the first intersection take the high road. Pass more cottages. Pick up Manitou Trail on your right near where the fence stops. Follow Manitou along the bluff until you reach Arch Rock. Check out the scene at Arch Rock and then take the stairway up to the Nicolet Watch Tower. Pick up Tranquil Bluff Trail and follow it along the bluff.

When you reach the small green electric company box labeled "caution," pick up Leslie Avenue, the paved road to your left, and continue in the same direction, paralleling the bluff. Turn left on Murray Trail (marked with a brown post), taking it to Crooked Tree Road, which is gravel. Turn left on Crooked Tree Road and follow it past the North Bicycle Trail, to its end. Turn right on Sugar Loaf Road, also gravel, and follow it around Sugar Loaf to the first intersection. Turn right onto Rifle Range Road and follow it a short distance.

Go up the stairway on your right to Fort Holmes. Explore Fort Holmes, then take Fort Holmes Road to Morning Snack Trail and turn right. This is an excellent area to see spring wildflowers. Turn left on Beechwood

The best way to see the island's trails is from the back of a horse.

Trail, follow it to the end, and then go left on Garrison Road. Go past the cemeteries, staying left at the paved intersection. Pass Skull Cave and then bear right. Bear right again and pass the Avenue of Flags at Fort Mackinac. Turn left at the Governor's summer residence and take Fort Street back to Marquette Park.

HORSEBACK RIDING

Many who know the island well claim the best way to experience it is from the back of a horse. Few places in the country are so geared to horseback riding.

Rental horses are available from the following stables:
- Cindy's on Market Street between Astor and Hoban, 847-3572
- Chambers on Market Street and Cadotte Avenue, 847-6231
- Jack's on Mahoney Avenue between Cadotte and Lake Shore Drive, 847-3391

Rental fees are about $22 per hour. All horses are rented with western tack, and guides are generally provided. It is best to go early in the day when the horses are fresh and so are you. Wear sensible clothing to protect your legs from rubbing on the saddle, and plan to take at least two hours. It takes that long to feel comfortable on your horse and see the terrain.

All the stables will escort you up the Grand Hill, so you should plan your route accordingly. For there, the summer homes at the Annex, Allouez Trail, and Fort Holmes are all pleasant destinations. If you have more time, you may want to explore Leslie Avenue, Crooked Tree Road, or Soldier's Garden.

On the way back, let your horses walk back to the barn so they arrive cooled down and ready for the next trip.

JOGGING

With over 140 miles of road and trails on Mackinac Island, the number of jogging routes just doesn't quit. But try one of these:

Round the Rock *(about eight miles)*. One lap around the perimeter of the island is 8.2 miles of level, paved ground with the constant opportunity to cool off in the lake. Morning or early evening is best for this route so you don't have as much bicycle traffic to contend with.

Arch Rock Climb *(about three miles)*. Beginning at Marquette Park, run east along the shore road past Mission Point Resort to the Arch Rock stairway. Run up the stairs to Arch Rock (count 'em; I think there are 177!). Take Arch Rock Road, which is the main paved road on your left when your back is to Arch Rock. Follow this to Huron Road and turn left. Follow Huron in front of the East Bluff cottages, and turn left at Mission Hill. At the bottom of the hill turn right on the shore road to return to Marquette Park.

ROLLERBLADING

The island's level, paved surfaces make it a favorite for in-line skaters. Because of the traffic downtown, in-line skating is not allowed in the commercial center. Watch for the line across the pavement on the lake shore road east of downtown near Mission Point Resort and west of downtown near Mahoney Avenue. Rollerblade away from town from either of these locations.

Bring your own skates and safety equipment or rent it from:
- Mission Point Resort, 906/847-3312
- Mackinac Outfitters, on the water in the shops near the marina, 906/847-6100

Rental rates are about $6 per hour.

SAILING

The Straits area is wonderful place to sail, and a stroll past the marina will whet your appetite. If you have your own sailboat, enjoy it. If you don't, check with the Chamber of Commerce to see if there's currently a charter sailboat service. They seem to come and go.

SCUBA

The Department of Natural Resources has named portions of the Straits area a bottomlands preserve, protecting it from alteration. There are a number of shipwrecks in the area, including the *Cedarville,* a 588-foot self-unloader built in 1927, whose hull is in 35 feet of water. For a deeper dive, the schooner *M. Stalker,* built in 1863, lies in 80 feet of water.

For more information, contact the Straits Scuba Center during the season at 906/643-7009 or year round at 810/558-9922.

STONE SKIPPING

A serious sport on Mackinac Island, stone skipping here requires skill. Waves interfere, and with millions of stones on the beaches, a discerning eye is needed to choose the right one for skipping. Rumor has it that the hard-core skippers go to Round Island to get the smoothest stones.

Each July 4th, masters and amateurs gather at Windermere Point for a tense showdown to determine who will be the year's International Stone Skipping and Gerplunking Champion. Traditionally, the winning skip is 25 or more.

Practice in this particular sport can take place anywhere on the water's edge, but the water is usually calmest between British Landing and Mission Point. Don't hit a swimmer!

SWIMMING

The sparkling waters of Lake Huron and the Straits of Mackinac are inviting if the weather is warm and you like very cold water. Water temperatures average 50 degrees in June and warm to about 70 degrees by August. Plan for the rocky surface and wear water shoes.

Favorite swimming spots include the end of the boardwalk on the west end of town, the British Landing area, the Arch Rock area, and the cove at Mission Point. The water generally gets deep very gradually, except at Mission Point where there's a rapid drop off and the freighters moving through the Straits can cause sudden currents. Swimming near the boat docks or off Windermere Point is dangerous and not recommended.

For sunbathers, Mission Point cove is the most comfortable, as you can settle down on the lawn and still be near the water. In all the other locations, you have to contend with the island's limestone heritage. If you'd rather watch people than freighters while you bronze, you'll be in good company at Marquette Park.

The following hotels have pools for their guests' use: Chippewa, Grand, Island House (indoors), Lake View (indoors), Mission Point Resort, and Stonecliffe. If your hotel doesn't have a pool and it's a perfect pool day, you can indulge at the Grand's pool and surrounding grounds for a daily per person charge.

TENNIS

Three good sets of tennis courts exist on Mackinac Island, and two are connected to hotels. None of the courts have lights.

The public courts are located behind Fort Mackinac in the woods off the South Bicycle Trail. Because they are tucked among the cedar trees, these courts are out of the wind and somewhat shaded. They are well maintained and free. There is sometimes a wait for one of the three courts, but by general consensus, courts are turned over to waiting players after one hour of play.

Mission Point Resort's courts are free for its guests and the public. The Grand Hotel has four wonderful clay courts that are available to guests and the public. Call the hotel at 906/847-3331 to inquire about rates and reserve a court. If you arrived on the island sans your racquet, rentals are available from Mission Point or the Grand.

VITA COURSE

The Grand Hotel has a half-mile vita course near the tennis and swimming area. It combines a jogging trail and exercise stations. The entrance to the first station is by the hotel's tennis shop on the Grand Hill.

WEIGHT LIFTING

Mission Point Resort has a health club for its guests' use, with free weights, weight machines, exercise bicycles, a sauna, and a steam room.

Rainy Days

It won't rain during your Mackinac Island excursion, I promise. But in case it does, here are ten things you could do on the island on a rainy day.

Take a carriage tour. The horses don't mind getting wet, and you'll stay dry while seeing the sights.

Spend the day at the Grand Hotel. Pay your admission fee and then enjoy. There is fine indoor shopping, eating, people-watching, and an opulent, turn-of-the-century feel.

Explore the Indian Dormitory. It's close to town and all the exhibits are indoors.

Go to the library. It has a whole room dedicated to documents about the island and its history. The chairs are comfortable and the fireplace and the view inviting.

Go fishing. I hear it's great in the rain.

Go to Mission Point Resort. There will probably be a fire in at least one of the five fireplaces, and an abundance of books on the shelves that invite browsing.

Go shopping downtown. You can dart between awnings and stay fairly dry. Because there are fewer people on the island when it rains, the shops are less crowded. Have a contest and see who can find the tackiest souvenir!

Sit on the front porch of a hotel. Sip hot coffee or cocoa, and listen to the sound of the foghorn guiding ships through the channel.

Conduct your own fudge taste test. Buy samples from each of the fudgemakers and decide for yourself which is the best.

Play a game. This is a perfect time to brush up on your Monopoly or Clue skills.

And take heart. Island insiders love rainy days. There are fewer people and the pace is even slower than usual.

11

Getting Attached

It happens; people fall in love with this island called Mackinac. Students come up for a summer job and never leave. Visitors return year after year. Couples get married on the island and return every anniversary. People wait for their dream house to come up for sale.

If you feel the fever, read on. There are many ways to have an intimate relationship with Mackinac Island.

Romantic Encounters

If you want to capture some romantic moments on Mackinac, try the following:
- Call one of the private livery carriage companies and arrange for a moonlight tour. Take your own late-night snack and beverage and tell the driver you aren't interested in any narration.

- Take a hike to Sunset Rock and watch the sun set. Sunset Rock is an out-of-the-way place on the Stonecliffe Resort property that reeks of romanticism. To get there, go to Stonecliffe by foot or taxi, and walk across the back lawn of the mansion to find a path to the apple orchard. Go through the orchard, turn right at the bluff path, and you're there.

- Go to Fort Holmes to watch the stars. Fort Holmes is the highest point on the island, and Mackinac Island night skies are unbelievably beautiful on a clear night. With luck you'll see the northern lights.

St. Anne's church is one of four churches available for summer weddings on the island.

- Stroll the boardwalk. Sit and listen to the waves lapping against the shore. Take off your shoes and socks and wade in the cold water. It is extra special on foggy nights, when you can hear the eerie sound of the foghorn and the chug-chug of a freighter's motor, but can only see dim lights when the freighter passes.

- Take a picnic to Brown's Brook. On the western side of the island, before you get to British Landing, Brown's Brook is an easy bike ride from downtown. Park your bikes and walk up next to the brook from the shore to find a wonderful fresh spring falling out of the limestone across rocks. From this vantage point, you can watch the cyclists going by, unaware of the treasure you have found.

- Rent a tandem bike. This encounter may be risky to suggest, because a bicycle built for two can challenge any relationship. But it's fun, and it's a good test: Can your relationship manage one set of handle bars and two sets of pedals? Give it a try.

- If you pass the tandem test, get married! Mackinac Island's popularity as a place to get married has exploded in recent years, and the hotels, restaurants, and related businesses are ready if you are. Start by contacting the Mackinac Island Chamber of Commerce (800/4LILACS, 906/847-6418, P.O. Box 451, Mackinac Island, MI 49757, or www.mackinac.com) and ask them to send you the *Mackinac Island Wedding Guide*. It's filled with stories and photographs of island weddings and has a comprehensive list of wedding planners, facilities, and other services.

Summer Jobs

Summer employees make the island work. About 3,500 of them come every year, seeking relaxation, good times, and money. The good times and the relaxation are almost guaranteed, as is hard work. The money depends on the job and the individual. The bulk of the workers are college age. Most of the jobs are in restaurants, hotels, and shops. Wages are typically minimum, except for tipping positions, which pay less than minimum. Housing is the biggest hassle and expense. Employers generally provide housing and deduct the cost from the employee's paycheck.

Workers usually work six long days a week during the peak season. Some don't make it past July 4th when they realize the work is hard, and it is a long way from home. Others come back year after year, enjoying the camaraderie and the locale. Businesses have a hard time keeping workers until the end of the season, so many offer bonuses to those who stay.

If you are interested in summer employment, contact the Chamber of Commerce for more information. They will provide you with a list of employers, and a brochure describing what to expect. It's best to inquire in the fall or winter. Some employers also list job openings on-line (www.mackinac.com).

Longer Stays

There are some options for those who would enjoy a longer stay on the island. Check Chapter Four for a list of condominiums and apartments that have weekly rates. The market for rental of historic cottages changed recently when the City Council passed a ruling related to fire and other regulations. The upshot is that most home owners have stopped renting their cottages or will only rent for a month or more at a time. Call Mackinac Island Realty (906/847-6483) for information, or check the *Town Crier* for advertisements.

Staying for Good

If you are really hooked, check out the real estate market. Stop in at Mackinac Island Realty's office on Market Street (conveniently located next to the bank) and drool, or call them at 906/847-6483.

*Home prices have escalated somewhat since this house
was built in 1885 for $2,000.*

If building your dream house is in the plan, you'll be happy to know that there are a number of vacant lots in the Stonecliffe area, some overlooking the Woods golf course. If your dreams include waterfront property, inquire about Stonebrook, which is about two miles from town. The newest development on the island is Trillium Heights, near Great Turtle Park.

Condominiums at Stonecliffe and other areas are sometimes available, starting at around $150,000. Ownership at Stonecliffe offers the benefit of property management, helping to defray cost of ownership.

The market for the older, historic homes is very tight. Many of the cottages are handed down through families, or snatched up before they really are listed for sale. When available, cottages start in the $350,000 range, and go up-up-up from there.

Conventions and Group Travel

If you want to bring your business associates to the island, or plan a class reunion or other event, do it. The island's relaxing atmosphere provides a great backdrop for business or social outings. The Grand Hotel, Mission Point Resort, and Lake View Hotel are good potential convention sites, with meeting space and experts on hand to help you with planning. A number of the other hotels have one or two meeting rooms available if your group is small. All the hotels have group rates.

Staying in Touch

The best way to stay in touch with what is happening on Mackinac Island is to subscribe to the island newspaper, the *Town Crier* (906/847-3788). The *Town Crier* is published weekly during the season and periodically during the off-season. Subscriptions can be purchased at the newspaper offices on Market Street, or by writing to *Town Crier*, P.O. Box 532, Mackinac Island, MI, 49757. Individual issues are sold out of stands on the island, and at the hotels.

Getting Involved

There are many ways to get involved with island activities during or after your stay. See the *Town Crier* for weekly events, and stop in on a few. A number of organizations have been created to funnel money and energy into important island activities. Some of the more active groups are:

Mackinac Associates. Founded by the Mackinac Island State Park Commission, this group acts as a friends organization to support the projects of the Commission. It is funded through memberships and through private contributions. Mackinac Associate members enjoy free entrance to any of the MISPC historical attractions, discounts on all purchases in the Fort stores, and the knowledge that they are contributing to the preservation of history in the Straits area. Write to Mackinac Associates, Box 370, Mackinac Island, MI 49757 for more information.

Mackinac Island Recreation and Development. MIRD's goal is to improve the recreational facilities on the island for year-round residents and summer visitors. MIRD is funded by contributions and the sale of an island calendar. MIRD is responsible for creating Great Turtle Park, a recreational area in the island's interior that includes a softball field, basketball court, playground equipment, and an equestrian ring. There are plans, big plans, for a swimming pool and community recreation area at the public school. Meanwhile, they need to sell more calendars. To get membership information or order a calendar contact MIRD (P.O. Box 421, Mackinac Island, MI 49757 906/847-6293). If you'd like, you can order a calendar online at www.mackinac.com.

Friends of the Mackinac Island Medical Center. This organization seeks contributions to offset the operating expense of the Mackinac Island Medical Center. For 30 years, they've produced a cookbook of recipes from island insiders and businesses. To get membership information or order a cookbook, stop in at the center, write P.O. Box 536, Mackinac Island, MI, 49757, or call 906/847-3583. Cookbooks can also be ordered through www.mackinac.com.

Special Reminders

To help you stay attached to Mackinac after you leave, shop for a special reminder of your island vacation:

A book about the island. Two all-star books are *Mackinac Island: Its History in Pictures* and *100 Years at Mackinac*. An old favorite, *Mackinac: The Gathering Place,* is out of print, so if you find a copy somewhere, snatch it quickly.

Fudge. Preferably several pounds, in a variety of flavors. Take home twelve pounds, put it in the freezer and take one pound out a month to remind you of your visit.

An island calendar. Mackinac Island Recreation and Development publishes a calendar each year featuring fine photographs of the island. People from all over the country submit photos, and the winners are selected during the island's Winter Festival. The calendars are sold at most island shops or see the information on page 123 to contact MIRD directly.

Photograph, print or a painting with an island theme. There are lots of these available, and they are lasting remembrances of your trip.

Sweatshirt, T-shirt, or hat with Mackinac written somewhere. With the variety available, it could take you all day to pick the right one.

Horseshoe. Where the horse is king, what could be a better remembrance or good luck charm?

Island duffel bag. The Grand Hotel shops carry these, with the horse and carriage logo. Very pricey, but very stylish. If you use one of these for airline travel, you will be amazed at how many people come up to you at baggage claim and share Mackinac stories.

Old-style photos. Two photo places dress you up like pioneers or dance-hall girlies and spit out a brown tone photo that looks like it was made at the turn of the century. Very fun.

The bridge should not be called "Big Mac."

Acting Like a Local

With a little coaching, it isn't hard for a visitor to pass as a local. Here are some tongue-in-cheek suggestions, taken from my dad Hugh McVeigh's treatise called "What You Always Wanted to Know about Mackinac Island but were Afraid to Ask."

- Never pronounce the island's name Mack-i-nack. The "nac" is pronounced "naw." Never spell the island's name Mackinaw, or the city on the mainland's name Mackinac. Mackinac Island and Mackinaw City are correct. The bridge is spelled with a final c.

- Bring your own bike to the island and buy a Mackinac Island bike license at the Police Station. This is an obvious badge of belonging. Riding on a rental bike is very "fudgie." If you have a fold-up bike, there isn't much you can do. You are obviously a boater.

- On the ride to the island, always go to the back of the boat, stretch out and act bored. Never look at the bridge or at passing freighters.

- Don't call the bridge the "Big Mac." Never wave at people on passing ferry boats.

- Hide your camera and your fudge.

- Always ride your licensed bike to the right, and give horses the right-of-way.

- Wear blue jeans that have a worn inner seam near the calf from constant exposure to bicycle gears.

- At night, act unconcerned about the bats even if they terrify you.

- Buy a bag of groceries from Doud's and carry it around all day.

- Never look up at the Fort when they shoot the cannon.

- Carry a backpack or a fanny pack, but never a purse.

- Call the Chippewa Hotel the Chip, the Village Inn the V.I., and the French Outpost the O.P.

Winter Wonderland

"The words I would use about winter are 'quiet' and 'peaceful.' We get our home back. I don't mean that as a slur on the tourists, because come spring we are ready for everyone to come back and for all the activity to begin again. I guess you'd say I can't wait for it [the summer season] to end and can't wait for it to begin." Jessie Doud, owner of Jesse's Chuck Wagon, echoed many year-round residents' sentiment when she made this statement to the island newspaper, the *Town Crier*.

Many people believe the island just closes up after the season. But that's not so. There's a vibrant year-round community here and a growing winter travel business.

About 600 people make Mackinac Island their year-round home. Most of them are descendants of the early Straits area Indian and French residents. Most of the permanent homes are in Harrisonville in the center of the island and at Stonecliffe near the airport.

From the time the last Arnold boat stops running January 2 until the ice bridge between the island and St. Ignace freezes (usually in February, but sometimes not at all), the only way to get on or off the island is by plane. When the ice bridge freezes, islanders mark the trail with Christmas trees and it becomes a winter highway, with snowmobilers, skiers, and walkers making the trip

In the winter, the island is usually blanketed with snow.

frequently. The ice bridge usually thaws in late March, and boat service resumes in May.

The island children attend school at the Mackinac Island public school, which has about ninety students, kindergarten through twelfth grade. There's no bus service. They ride their bikes as long as possible, and then snowmobiles become the primary mode of transportation.

The island residents spend their winter catching up with friends and family that they didn't have much time to see during the busy summer season, preparing buildings and businesses for the next season, relaxing, and traveling. The Mustang Lounge, the Village Inn, and St. Anne's Church become the centers of social activity.

The island's hiking trails and carriage roads make beautiful cross-country ski trails. The snow is unspoiled by automobile exhaust, and because snowmobiles are restricted from many areas, the snow is pristine.

If you are an adventurer, explore Mackinac in the winter. Some of the bed and breakfasts are open year-round, while others open for particular dates, such as Christmas, New Year's, and the Winter Festival. Contact the Chamber of Commerce year-round for more information (800/4-LILACS, 906/847-6418, or P.O. Box 451, Mackinac Island, MI 49757).

"My favorite way to spend a day on Mackinac is cross-country skiing after a 24-hour snow storm when the trees are weighed down with a foot of snow and there is no sign of any other humans.

My advice for the first-time visitor: (1) bring comfortable walking shoes and clothing; and (2) be patient, part of the beauty of Mackinac is the pace."

–Melinda Porter
Long-time island resident

12

Native Knowledge

At this point, if you have faithfully read *Mackinac Connection* chapter by chapter, you will be a well informed visitor. The following alphabetized list will help you take the final steps toward becoming an insider.

ADDRESSES
There aren't any. This drives UPS and Federal Express crazy, so we make them up, like 1001 Stonecliffe Road. The truth is that all mail goes to boxes at the post office, where it is picked up by island residents. When a UPS or Federal Express package arrives, the dray driver delivers it based on his or her own knowledge. Directions are given by major landmark.

AIRPORT
Mackinac Island Airport is a paved, lighted, 3,500 foot airstrip in the center

There are over 2,500 bicycles on the island in the summer.

of the island. See Chapter Three for more information, or call 906/847-3231.

ARCADE GAMES
Arcade games are available at the Star Line dock, the Island House, Mission Point Resort, and the Grand Hotel.

BATS
Spend an evening on Mackinac Island and you'll likely meet a real native, the island bat. Bats are more afraid of you than you are of them, so don't be concerned. The bats are major mosquito eaters, and are a reason the

island is free of those critters. When we were kids, major entertainment used to be scaring bats out of buildings on Main Street and then watching the tourists cower. We're reformed, I promise.

BANKS

There are two banks on Mackinac Island, and both of them have outdoor ATM machines. The First National Bank of St. Ignace on Market Street was the only game in town for as long as most of us can remember. The new kid on the block is North County Bank and Trust around the corner by the Village Inn. If you find yourself short on cash, stop in.

BICYCLE AUCTION

For an unusual shopping experience, attend the Mackinac Island bicycle auction held at the Police Station on Market Street on the second Saturday in June. Over 200 bicycles that have been impounded and not claimed, or simply abandoned, are auctioned off to the public, usually at rock-bottom prices.

BICYCLE FLAGS

Bicycle flags can scare horses. Take yours off, or wrap the flag around the pole and secure it.

BICYCLE REPAIRS

If you bring your bike to the island and find it a bit flat, or cranky, stop in at the Island Bike Shop just east of the marina. They have mechanics on duty seven days a week to keep you cycling. Call 847-6337 for more information.

CAMPING

No. Camping is not allowed anywhere on Mackinac Island. There are campgrounds in Mackinaw City and St. Ignace. Contact their Chambers of Commerce for information.

CHAMBER OF COMMERCE

The Mackinac Island Chamber of Commerce is located on Main Street between Fort and Astor, on the north side. The friendly folks there can answer almost any questions you might have about the island. The size of the building belies the size of the business the Chamber does. Calls come in from all over the world, and packets of information are mailed throughout the year.

To reach the Mackinac Island Chamber year-round:
Call 800/4LILACS or 906/847-6418
Write P.O. Box 451, Mackinac Island, MI 49757
Surf www.mackinac.com or www.mackinacislchamber.org

To reach the Mackinaw City Chamber:
Call 800/666-0160 or 616/436-5574
Write P.O. Box 856, Mackinaw City, MI 49710
Surf www.mackinawcity.com

The Mackinac Island Chamber of Commerce is open
9:00 a.m. to 6:00 p.m. daily in the summer.

To reach the St. Ignace Chamber:
Call 800/338-6660 or 906/643-8717
Write 11 State Street, St. Ignace, MI 49781
Surf www.stignace.com

CHURCHES
There are three churches operating on the island. Call for service times, or check the *Town Crier*.

St. Anne's Catholic–Huron and Church Streets, just east of downtown
847-3507

Trinity Episcopal–On Fort Street, just past Market
847-3798

Little Stone Congregational–On Cadotte Avenue, at the base of the Grand Hotel Hill
847-3877

DRAYS
Horse-drawn drays are the primary method of moving freight on the island. They are the equivalent of flat-bed trucks, only the horsepower is different. Drays move everything that is moveable, from produce to fuel oil. Call 847-6174.

ELECTRICITY
Huge underwater cables bring electricity to the island from generators on the mainland operated by the Edison Sault Electric Company. Many places on the island are heated with by electric heat.

FIRE
The island has an all-volunteer fire department and one motorized fire truck. When the alarm starts howling, fire fighters drop what they are doing, hop on their bicycles, and head to the Fire Station. The Fire Department emergency phone is 847-3344.

If you want to build a fire to roast your marshmallows on the beach, you must get a permit from the police.

FLORISTS
The Grand Hotel has a florist shop that delivers beautiful arrangements anywhere on the island. Call 847-3331. Mission Point Resort (847-3312) and the Chippewa Hotel (847-6440) recently added florist shops as well.

FUDGIES
The name given to day tourists by islanders. Fudgies are usually identified by the cameras around their necks and the pound of fudge in their hands.

GOVERNMENT
The island has two governing bodies: the City of Mackinac Island and the Mackinac Island State Park Commission. They work together to ensure that the island successfully makes its transition every year from an isolated small town of 600 people to a major tourist destination.

The City of Mackinac Island is run by a mayor and a city council. It has responsibility for municipal services (water, sewer, and waste), police and fire protection, and maintenance of the city streets, cemeteries, and city-owned buildings. The City generates income through property taxes, business and transportation permits, and fees paid by ferry companies based on a percentage of their revenue.

The Mackinac Island State Park Commission is a commission appointed by the governor that has responsibility for the state park land (80 percent of the island), including the historic buildings, trails, roads, airport, and land leases. The MISPC has a small year-round staff, and offices at Fort Mackinac and in Lansing, Michigan. The state operations on the island are funded through proceeds from ticket sales at historic buildings, sale of revenue bonds, and state appropriations.

HAIR SALON
If you find yourself having a "bad hair day," the Grand Hotel (906/847-3331) and Mission Point Resort (906/847-3312) have hair salons.

HUNTING
Hunting is not allowed on Mackinac Island. Basically, there is nothing to hunt anyway. One year, a cottage owner raised turkeys in his barn and let them loose when he left for his winter home. Island people fed the confused flock the first winter and they survived, raised babies, and learned to fly up in the trees to avoid dogs. But they have disappeared.

ICE BRIDGE
Most winters, the waters freeze between British Landing or the Stonecliffe area on the island and St. Ignace, providing an ice bridge or winter highway. The bridge usually forms in February and lasts through March, and residents travel it on foot, cross-country skis, or snow machines (see page 138).

ISLAND TIME
A term affectionately used by insiders to describe Mackinac Island's own set of priorities and timing. Island time takes a little while to get used to. Then it becomes the reason you are here.

LAUNDRY
There are laundromats above the Dockside Restaurant on the west end of town, and near Bay View Cottage east of the marina. These spots are very popular with summer employees, so plan to spend several hours.

LIBRARY
The Mackinac Island Library was recently moved from a small, dark location on Market Street to a lovely new building on the waterfront. The reading room has a fireplace and outdoor decks to accommodate the reader. Current newspapers from the Midwest are on the racks, as well as magazines. The library is on Windermere Point, at the western end of town. Call 847-3421 for hours.

Library cards are for anyone who will be on the island four weeks or more. Others are welcome to use the facilities, including the low-cost computer internet access and children's computer. Also popular is the continuous used book sale where visitors and residence can drop off the books they've finished and pick up new ones at a minimal charge.

LIGHTHOUSES
There are two lighthouses visible from Mackinac Island. The Round Island lighthouse is the original, built in 1895 complete with a keeper's apartment, and used continuously for 52 years. It was replaced in 1947 by the space-age white automatic beacon near the break wall.

LILACS
June is Lilac time on Mackinac Island. If your timing is right, you'll be able to smell the lilacs as you approach the harbor. Most of the lilacs were imported to the island by the French Jesuits who wanted a little of their native flora. There are more than 400 varieties of lilacs, from whites to pale lavender to pink to deep purples. Some of the original Jesuit trees are over 300 years old; these aren't bushes, they are trees with wonderfully gnarled trunks.

LIQUOR
Doud's grocery store has the only full-service package liquor store on the island. The Grand Hotel also has some liquor in their gift shop. The drinking age in Michigan is 21.

LITTER

Don't do it. Mackinac Island's attractiveness comes from its natural beauty. Respect it. If you take a picnic to the woods, and can't spy a litter barrel, take the stuff back to town and put it in a waste container.

LOCKERS

If you brought more gear than you can carry, small lockers are available near the Star Line dock and at the Shepler dock, on the west end of town.

LOTTERY

State of Michigan lottery tickets are available at Doud's grocery store.

MACKINAC BRIDGE

The Mackinac Bridge is a five-mile long suspension bridge that connects Michigan's upper and lower peninsulas between Mackinaw City and St. Ignace. It was completed in 1957, after three years of difficult construction. The continual maintenance is funded through tolls. Each year on Labor Day, Michigan's Governor leads thousands of walkers on a hike across the bridge.

Learn more about the bridge on the Internet: www.mackinacbridge.com.

Over 800,000 people come to Mackinac Island every year.

MEDICAL

The Mackinac Island Medical Center is on Market Street near the Post Office. If you need medical attention, call 847-3582 during the day or 847-3962 evenings or weekends, or stop by. The Center is staffed by a doctor, two residents, a nurse, and an X-ray technician during the summer. The doctors are on rotation from Beaumont Hospital near Detroit.

The Center is equipped to handle most island incidents (bike accidents are the most common problem) but for more serious situations, patients may be transported to the mainland by boat or airplane. Ambulance service is run by Lifelink, Inc. assisted by a team of volunteer Emergency Medical Technicians. For medical emergencies, call 847-3344.

MOVIES

For a real local experience, attend the Monday night movie at the Mission Point Resort theater. You'll see flyers around town advertising the feature of the week. They are all first-run films, due to the kindness of the Loek's family who own Star Theaters and a home on the island. There is an admission charge. The Grand Hotel also periodically has movies for its guests.

Two full-length motion pictures have been made on Mackinac Island. The first was *This Time for Keeps*, starring Esther Williams and Jimmy Durante in 1946. *Somewhere in Time*, starring Christopher Reeves, Jane Seymour, and Christopher Plummer, was filmed in 1979. Many of the locals were extras in the movie. The movie lives on with quite a loyal following. Every fall, the Grand Hotel has a Somewhere in Time weekend, where guests dress the parts, meet with movie talent, and relive the experience.

The island has a full motion picture sound stage at Mission Point Resort, which was built by Moral Re-Armament to produce MRA promotional films, and is currently used for special events.

NEWSPAPERS

The island paper, the *Town Crier*, is published weekly during the summer and periodically through the winter. Copies are available in newsstands throughout town.

More sophisticated but less interesting papers are available from Alford's Drug Store, the Island Book Store, and the hotels.

Mackinac Island is a great family vacation destination.

PLAYGROUNDS
There are three: behind the Indian Dormitory, at the island school off the boardwalk on the west end of town, and at Great Turtle Park in the interior of the island.

PHOTO PROCESSING
Same-day photo processing is available at Photos on Market on Market Street. Benjamin's and the Picture Shop on Main Street will send your photos off the island to be developed with a longer turnaround time.

POLICE

Mackinac Island has four year-round police officers. About five additional officers and two state troopers join the force for the summer season. The most common crimes are alcohol-related and bicycle theft. The police station has a two-cell jail. The Police station is located on Market Street by the Post Office. Call 847-3344 to reach the police.

POST OFFICE

The Post Office is on Market Street. Just take the sidewalk up from the Main Street beside the Chamber of Commerce. They have Saturday hours during the season. Also, if you are expecting express mail, leave your phone number by calling them at 847-3821, so they'll know where to reach you. All residents have boxes and pick up their mail, as there is no direct mail delivery.

RASPBERRIES

Delicious tiny wild raspberries grow in many of the island meadows. Look for them in mid-August just past the end of the airport runway.

REST ROOMS

Public rest rooms are located:
- Behind the Chamber of Commerce office on Main Street in the middle of downtown
- Inside the Visitor's Center across from Marquette Park
- Near the Star Line dock on the west end of town
- At Arch Rock
- At British Landing

REVEILLE

At 9:00 a.m., be prepared for the uplifting sounds of reveille coming from Fort Mackinac.

ROCK

A not-so-affectionate term used for Mackinac Island by insiders who need a mainland fix. As in "I need to get off this rock."

ROLLER BLADING

You can bring your blades to the island and take advantage of the paved, flat surfaces. But don't skate near downtown. West of town near the boardwalk there's a sign and a line painted across the street. Skate away from town from that point or look for similar markings on the pavement east of town near Mission Point Resort. There's just too much traffic near downtown to skate safely. See page 114 for information on rentals.

SCHOOL
The island has one school, housing kindergarten through 12th grade. There are usually about 90 students and ten teachers, a ratio most parents would love. High school graduating classes number about five. Team sports in the high school take place under the name "the Lakers," part of the Northern Lights League. As you can imagine, they don't play football.

SCOUTS
The Mackinac Island State Park Commission conducts a program to bring scouting troops to the island for a week of recreation and assistance. A different troop comes to the island each week in the summer, stays in the barracks near Fort Mackinac, and performs various duties to help in the historical attractions.

Interested troop leaders should contact the commission the summer before they are interested in participating in the program. (Mackinac Island State Park Commission, P.O. Box 370, Mackinac Island, MI 49757.)

SIZE
Mackinac Island is about 2,200 acres, and is 8.2 miles around. It is three miles long.

SKATE BOARDS
No.

SNOW MACHINES
Island-speak for snowmobiles, snow machines are the primary mode of transport in the winter.

STREET SWEEPERS
The invaluable service provided by the street sweepers often goes unnoticed. By hand and broom and wheelbarrow these good folks keep the manure swept up off the streets. They are employed by the city, the State Park, and the Grand Hotel.

STROLLERS
Strollers can be rented from Ryba's (847-6261) or Orr Kids' (847-321) bicycle rental shops.

TAPS
The evening sign-off at the Fort is signalled by the playing of taps at 10:00 p.m. It's so predictable, some cottagers use it as a signal to their children to be home.

TAXI

Taxis are horse-drawn carriages dispatched by radio control. The magic number is 847-3323. The magic word is patience. The taxi company will do its best to be on time. Plan on a wait.

TELEPHONES

Pay phones are located in most of the hotels and all the boat docks. There are also public phones at the marina, Chamber of Commerce, City Hall, Grand Hotel golf course, and British Landing.

TRASH

In 1992, the island's landfill closed, and a new waste management program was launched. Residents and businesses are required to separate trash that can be recycled, trash that can be composted, and trash that needs to be sent to a landfill off the island. Special trash bags are purchased that indicate which kind of trash is contained. Blue bags are the most expensive, and everything can be put in blue bags. Beige bags are a third of the cost and can only contain compostable items. Recyclables are free, if boxes are broken down and tied, and cans and bottles are clean.

VIDEO RENTAL

Doud's grocery store (847-3551) has a collection of 200 videos available for rental as well as a limited number of VCRs. The library also has videos.

WATER

The island uses Lake Huron as its water source. Water is treated at a plant just east of Mission Point and then stored near Fort Holmes. Waste water is treated at a sewage treatment plant near the airport.

WHEELCHAIRS

A limited number of wheelchair, adult stroller, and mobility cart rentals are available from Alford's Drug Store, Lake View Bikes, Orr Kids' Bikes, and Ryba's Bikes. The Visitor's Center and Star Line each have one wheelchair available on a first-come, first-served basis.

There is a taxi and a carriage tour that can accommodate a wheelchair, but arrangements need to be made in advance. Call 906/847-3307 for more information.

For more information about the accessibility of island accommodations and restaurants, contact the Mackinac Island Chamber of Commerce.

Additional Readings

For those who are interested in additional reading about Mackinac Island, there are numerous publications. Many of them served as useful sources for me.

Armour, David, *100 Years at Mackinac*, Mackinac Island State Park Commission, Mackinac Island, Mich., 1995.

Armour, David and Keith Widder, *At the Crossroads – Michilimackinac During the American Revolution*, Mackinac Island State Park Commission, Mackinac Island, Mich., 1978.

Fuller, Iola, *The Loon Feather*, Harcourt Brace Jovanich, Orlando, Fla., 1968.

Gringhuis, Dirk, *Lore of the Great Turtle: Indian Legends of Mackinac Retold*, Mackinac Island State Park Commission, Mackinac Island, Mich., 1970.

McCabe, John, *Grand Hotel: Mackinac Island*, The Unicorn Press, Lake Superior State College, Sault Ste. Marie, Mich., 1978.

McKee, Russell, editor, *Mackinac: The Gathering Place*, Michigan Natural Resources Magazine publication, Lansing, Mich., 1981.

Petersen, Eugene, *Mackinac Island: Its History in Pictures*, Mackinac Island State Park Commission, Mackinac Island, Mich., 1973.

Porter, Phil and Victor Nelhiebel, *The Wonder of Mackinac*, Mackinac Island State Park Commission, Mackinac Island, Mich., 1984.

Porter, Phil, *View from the Veranda*, Mackinac Island State Park Commission, Mackinac Island, Mich., 1981.

Rubin, Lawrence, *Mighty Mac*, Kiwanis Club of St. Ignace, St. Ignace, Mich., 1958.

Williams, Meade, *Early Mackinac*, Avery Color Studios, Au Train, Mich., 1987 reprint of an 1897 publication.

Widder, Keith, *Dr. Beaumont: The Mackinac Years*, Mackinac Island State Park Commission, Mackinac Island, Mich., 1975.

Wood, Edwin, *Historic Mackinac*, The MacMillan Company, New York, New York, 1918.

About the Author

Amy McVeigh started exploring Mackinac Island on her Shetland pony when she was six years old. Since then, she's ridden, hiked, biked, jogged, swam, and skied her way to every corner. She wrote *Mackinac Connection: The Insider's Guide to Mackinac Island* to help visitors enjoy the Mackinac Island that she and her family have discovered in more than twenty years summering on the island.

Amy lives in Beverly Hills, Michigan, with her husband Jeff Braun, and her two daughters, Jordan and Madison Braun.

Ordering Information

If you love this book, please don't loan it to anyone. Buy them a copy!

You can order *Mackinac Connection: The Insider's Guide to Mackinac Island* three ways:

- Ask your local bookstore to get you a copy if they don't have one in stock.
- If you are an internet user, order through www.amazon.com.
- Order directly from the publisher.

To order from the publisher, send a check or money order to:
Mackinac Publishing
P.O. Box 215
Mackinac Island, MI 49757

Price: $12.95 per book
Tax: $ .78 per book (Michigan residents only)
Shipping: $ 2.00 per book

Send a note indicating:
Your full name
Address (street, P.O. Box, apartment number, city, state, and zip code)
Phone number
Number of books you are ordering

Thank you!

INDEX